MW00717194

Suppressed History II

Pulverizing Politically Correct Paradigms

B. Forrest Clayton

First Edition

Armistead Publishing - Cincinnati, Ohio

Suppressed History II - 2

Suppressed History II
Pulverizing Politically Correct Paradigms
B. Forrest Clayton

Published by:
Armistead Publishing
P.O. Box 54516
Cincinnati, OH 45254

ISBN, print ed.   0-9723920-1-7
First Printing 2005
Printed in the United States of America

Suppressed History II - 3

Contents

Acknowledgements
About the Author

Bibliography

Acknowledgments

I dedicate this book to my mother, who is the greatest teacher I have ever known. She was a political science major who made an attempt to impart her expertise to me. She graduated from Smith College before women were allowed into the Ivy League. I would like to thank Ed Meese, the former Attorney General of the United States, for giving me an excellent endorsement for my first book. I would also like to acknowledge Tom Kilgannon and the other patriotic Americans at *Freedom Alliance* who so graciously allowed me to serve there as a visiting fellow. They can be found at FreedomAlliance.org. My sincere thanks to Joel Roadruck. While educating me about Intelligent Design one Sunday morning before Church, he also introduced me to the concept of Mokele Mbembe. I would also like to thank those who helped me with my website at *suppressedhistory.com*. I would like to thank all of you who read my first book and responded with notes of encouragement and with requests for more. I hope that my books help you in your quest for knowledge and in your journey to the truth. We need historical perspective. We need uncensored truth. We must explore the past in order to understand the present. As T.S. Eliot wrote, "We shall not cease from exploration and the end of all our exploring will be to arrive where we started and know the place for the first time."

About the Author

B. Forrest Clayton is also the author of
*Suppressed History: Obliterating Politically Correct
Orthodoxies*. He has appeared on many national
radio and television shows including MSNBC's
Scarborough Country and *The Michael Reagan
Show*. In addition, he has appeared in the
national print media, including the *New York
Times* and the international print media including
The London Times.

"During times of universal deceit, telling the truth becomes a revolutionary act."

George Orwell

1
Bias in the Media and Academia

*"Facts do not cease to exist because they are
ignored."*
– Aldous Huxley

The liberals in the media and academia try
to deceive the general public in order to promote
their leftwing ideology. Their favorite tactic in
their deceitful endeavor is not the outright lie of
commission, although they do resort to this on
occasion, but instead it is the subtle lie of
omission, which they utilize everyday. They know
that an outright lie is hard to deny, but the intent
behind an omission is plausibly deniable.

For there is a limited amount of time in a
collegiate lecture and in a nightly news broadcast.
There is a limited amount of space in a
newspaper. Frequently, the conscious or
unconscious liberal bias of the journalists and
professors manifests itself in what is omitted from
the lecture, broadcast, or newspaper. This book
is an attempt to fill in some of those gaps and to
reveal facts that were omitted because of liberal
bias.

Many conservative intellectuals believe that
conservative talk radio has done a magnificent job
countering the liberal political bias of the
mainstream news media in relation to current
events, but that it has failed to counter liberal
bias in such fields as history, music, art, science,
and religion. It has failed in these cultural areas
only because it has not tried. Most three-hour
conservative talk shows spend all three hours on

current political events and rarely ever delve deeper into history or culture. Current political events are like the water in a great river that merely flows down from its source. Their sources are the monumental mountains known as history and culture. Current political events are the branches and leaves on a tree. History and culture are the trunk and the roots. We must understand the source and the roots if we want to fully comprehend the river and the tree. We must understand the past in order to fully understand the present. This book is an attempt to pick up where conservative talk radio has left off.

Even many highly placed insiders in the media admit that there is a dominant liberal bias in the "mainstream" media. The "mainstream" news media as defined here includes *CBS, NBC, ABC, CNN*, the *New York Times*, and *The Washington Post*. Bernard Goldberg, who was a high-ranking official at *CBS News*, blew the whistle on liberal bias in the media when he wrote his book *Bias*. Andy Rooney of *CBS* News' *60 Minutes* program said that Bernard Goldberg "made some very good points" in his book on the media's liberal bias. Rooney said, "There is no question that I, among others, have a liberal bias." Then Andy Rooney let the cat out of the bag when he said, "I think Dan Rather is transparently liberal. Now he may not like to hear me say that. I always agree with him, too. But I think he should be more careful." Dan Rather should have taken Rooney's advice. In September of 2004, Dan Rather revealed his liberal bias when he put forth and stood behind forged documents in an attempt to destroy the presidency of George W. Bush.

Bernard Goldberg is not the only one to blow the whistle on liberal bias in the mainstream news media. *ABC*'s John Stossel who is the co-anchor of *20/20* said, "Where I live in Manhattan and where I work at *ABC*, people say *conservative* the way people say *child molester*. Leftist thinking is just the culture that I live in and the culture in which the reporters who populate the mainstream media live. Everybody just agrees: more safety regulations, more gun control, and higher taxes. Who could not want that? Everybody around here wants that. Anyone who disagrees is seen as not just wrong, but selfish and cruel. If I try to discuss this with my peers, I get blank stares. The press is so filled with hatred for capitalism that someone who advocates for free markets rather than government control is a conservative and a problem. The reason the *New York Times*, and to a lesser extent *The Washington Post*, are so important, and they are, is because the TV and radio copy them sycophantically. That is how bias at the *New York Times* becomes bias in other media."

A leading editor at the *New York Times* in 2004 acknowledged liberal bias in the *Times* reporting on the issues of homosexual "marriage" and abortion. He chastised his reporters for making their personal liberal bias on these issues transparent in their articles. He was not referring to the op-ed pages but the regular articles, which were supposed to report the news objectively. He told his reporters that their labeling of pro-abortion people as pro-choice and in the same article labeling anti-abortion people as anti-choice or anti-abortion as opposed to pro-life was inconsistent and biased. He told them to be more objective when writing about social issues.

In the year 2004, during a closely contested presidential campaign between George W. Bush and John F. Kerry, the political left censored and suppressed an anti-Kerry film entitled *Stolen Honor: Wounds That Never Heal.* The left said it would be unfair to Kerry, so they suppressed it. Of course they had no problem showing Michael Moore's anti-Bush film entitled *Fahrenheit 9-11.* The conservative film was suppressed. The liberal film was shown in theaters all over the country. The leftist was protected by the first amendment, but the POW war heroes in *Stolen Honor* were shutdown, censored, and suppressed.

Beware of the media-corporate-complex. For example, *Viacom* led by the leftist Mel Karmazan whose *MTV* exposed Janet Jackson's breast on national television during the Super Bowl halftime show, owns not only *MTV*, but also *CBS News* and *60 Minutes* and most of Howard Stern's radio stations. Karmazan has used *60 Minutes* to promote books that bash president Bush in an election year, frequently without giving full disclosure that a company owned and controlled by *Viacom* published those books. Karmazan has also utilized Howard Stern to attack Bush in an election year on a show that rarely deals with politics, but usually prefers to pander obscenity, indecency, and pornography.

Another example of the media corporate complex is Michael Eisner's *Disney Corporation*, which owns *ABC News* and the *History Channel.*

Eisner's subordinate Peter Jennings, the anchor at *ABC News*, banned, censored, and purged country music star Toby Keith from performing his song "Courtesy of the Red, White, and Blue" on an *ABC* television special after 9-11-01 because Jennings believed that Toby Keith's song was not politically correct. You see Toby Keith's song was pro-American and anti-terrorist in no uncertain terms, and that is deemed to be inappropriate by the leftists in the so-called "mainstream" news media. In their minds obscenity, indecency, and pornography are ok, but patriotic, conservative, political speech is taboo. Like Karmazan, Michael Eisner put forth a two-hour revisionist Alamo documentary on the *History Channel*, which promoted the politically correct, revisionist Alamo film by *Touchstone Pictures*, which was to come out shortly thereafter. The *History Channel* never gave full disclosure in that documentary that they were owned by the same corporation (*Disney*) that owned *Touchstone Pictures*. Not surprisingly, traditionalist Alamo scholars were excluded from the documentary. Only leftwing revisionists were included. These are interlocking directorates that deceive the public by posing as separate entities under separate names, and are "objectively" analyzing and reviewing books, films, news broadcasts etc. The truth is they have political and economic agendas that they are not disclosing.

Some may ask what is the impact of the liberal domination of the "mainstream" news media? A part of the impact is that many huge stories are virtually ignored. For example, the leftists in the news media have censored, omitted, and refused to cover the trials on the partial birth abortion ban act. Judge Richard Conway Casey in a New York courtroom allowed Dr. Kanwaljeet Anand, "An Oxford and Harvard trained neonatal pediatrician" to testify in April of 2004 to the fact that, "unborn children would feel 'excruciating pain' during either a dilation and evacuation or dilation and extraction abortion." "He said that by 20 weeks fetuses have developed all the nerve and brain functions to feel pain. Delivering the child up to its head, slicing open its skull and sucking out the brains would all produce 'prolonged and excruciating pain to the fetus'." John Dawson in *World* magazine, a conservative Christian publication, wrote, "The *New York Times* news room stands less than four miles from the courtroom, but the 'newspaper of record' has not sent a reporter to the courthouse since the trials started." These sad facts completely abolish the idea that the mainstream news media is objective and balanced in their reporting of the news. Remember, the *New York Times* did not lie about the partial birth abortion ban act trials; they just refused to cover them. Therefore, most of the rest of the media did not know they existed. This is an example of their favorite tactic: the lie of omission.

Liberals in the media claim that southern states should ban the Confederate Battle Flag, because they claim it represents slavery, even though only one in four Confederate soldiers owned a slave. That same news media says virtually nothing about slavery going on today in the African country of Sudan. See, in the Sudan today, the slavery is Black on Black. It is also Muslim on Christian. Arab Muslims are enslaving Christian Africans in the southern part of the Sudan. This is deemed to be wholly acceptable by the secular leftists in the American media. Therefore, this huge story is omitted or downplayed.

Another huge story omitted or downplayed by the leftists in the American media is the story unfolding in the African country of Zimbabwe. The black dictator of Zimbabwe, Robert Mugabe, sent armed gangs of black thugs to rape white women, kill their husbands, and steal their houses and farmland. Mugabe is a Marxist, who believes that the redistribution of wealth should not just take place through the slow and tedious procedure of high taxation, but instead through the rapid procedure of armed force. He believes all whites should be driven out of Zimbabwe (formerly Rhodesia) or killed. When these white women in Zimbabwe are raped by their black attackers, they fear it is a death sentence "because up to a third of sexually active Zimbabweans are infected with the AIDS virus." "In addition to the rape campaign, Zimbabwe's white farmers have been systematically murdered by radical blacks associated with the *Azania People's Organization*, or AZAPO, since 1994. The government of Robert Mugabe has winked at the farm seizures-and sometimes encouraged them." This violence against women is not shouted about and decried by the leading feminist organizations in America. This violence against women is not put forth as a "crisis" by the American news media. It is ignored because it is Black on White, and that is perfectly acceptable to the leftists who control much of the media as well as the *National Organization for Women.* (It should be re-named the *National Organization for Leftwing Women.*)

In 1994, 800,000 Rwandans were murdered, and president Bill Clinton and the U.S. news media stood by and did nothing to stop it. It was considered to be inconsequential by the leftwing elites in the American media and in the Clinton White House, because these white liberals could care less about the deaths of 800,000 blacks in Africa, as long as it was other black people who killed them. Many white liberals are racists to the core. President George W. Bush and columnist Walter E. Williams called it "the soft bigotry of low expectations". Many white liberals, because of their racist bigotry, don't expect blacks to be able to behave themselves in school, get good grades, and refrain from Black on Black crime. Therefore, white liberals push for affirmative action, to discriminate on the basis of race, and they ignore or downplay Black on Black crime. But as soon as a white police officer shoots or beats a black criminal and it is caught on tape, it becomes a national cause celebre among the media elite. It fits their paradigm of the evil white cop, the evil white South African farmer, the evil white middle class male, and it helps them to salve their guilty conscience for living the life of a limousine liberal and sending their children to overwhelmingly white exclusive private schools. Remember, when Bill Clinton lived in Washington D.C., he refused to send his daughter to the public schools. He sent Chelsea to an elite private school.

The secular left which controls the news media is not only racist; it is also anti-Semitic. The leftists in the news media are almost all anti-Israel and pro-Palestinian terrorism in their foreign policy views. They are always criticizing Israel and siding with the Muslim fanatics who send forth suicide bombers as if they were going out of style. It is the religious right that has been the most consistently pro-Israel in their foreign policy views. The greatest friends in the world the Jews in Israel have are the evangelical Christians in America. Michael Medved has made this point, but it has been virtually ignored by the mainstream media.

The Armenian Genocide of 1915 has been virtually ignored by the liberals in the media and academia. Why? Because Muslims were killing off Christians and the killing of Christians is deemed perfectly acceptable by the secular left. The Armenian Genocide of 1915 set an awful precedent. "In 1931, Hitler discussed with Richard Breiting the need for massive resettlements (deportations). He said, 'We intend to introduce a resettlement policy. Think of the biblical deportation and the massacres of the Middle Ages...and remember the extermination of the Armenians. One eventually reaches the conclusion that the masses of man are mere biological plasticine." Hitler went on to say, "Who, after all, speaks today of the annihilation of the Armenians?"

Back in 1915, the American Committee on Armenian Atrocities said, "As many as a million people had either been killed, relocated, or forced to renounce Christianity." Christians are being persecuted and killed all over the Muslim and Communist world today, but the secular leftists in the media do their best to censor these stories from their broadcasts. *Microsoft* was threatened by the Turkish Government because of their entry on the Armenian genocide of 1915 in their *Encarta* online encyclopedia. The Turkish government wants that portion of history suppressed. According to the *Harvard University Gazette*, "The Turkish government has threatened to prevent U.S. and British pilots from utilizing its air base for patrol flights over Northern Iraq if a resolution recognizing the role of the Ottoman Empire in the Armenian genocide passes." They want to suppress history so that Islam will always appear as a religion of peace and never as a religion of aggressive war on those who do not bow to the dictates of the Koran.

A few years before 9-11-01, Samuel Huntington wrote a book about what he termed the "Clash of Civilizations" between the militant Islamic East and the Judeo-Christian West. In 1993, Muslim militants detonated a bomb at the World Trade Center in New York City, which killed some people, but failed to bring the structure down. President Bill Clinton did not use massive military power to retaliate against Muslim terrorists who bombed the World Trade Center. Clinton thought he could appease the Muslim terrorists by militarily supporting Muslims over the Serbians in the Balkans, but this policy failed to appease the Muslim terrorists around the word. Bin Laden saw this as a sign of weakness, and on 9-11-01 his subordinates were successful in completely bringing down the twin towers of New York City's World Trade Center.

This secular leftwing bias not only exists in the news media, but also in the hallowed halls of academia. Most college professors are members of the secular left. David Horowitz felt the need to put forth an academic bill of rights in order to bring some semblance of balance to college campuses that lean overwhelmingly to the left. The *American Legion Magazine* in an article entitled "Academia versus America" stated that, "since the 1960's, universities have become havens for displaced radicals and political agitation." The *Luntz Survey* reported that 84% of Ivy League professors voted for Al Gore, 9% for George W. Bush, and 6% for Ralph Nader. The general public was split 48% Bush to 48% Gore. The professorship is tilted way left of center, vis a vis the American population as a whole. *American Enterprise* in September of 2002, in an article entitled, "Shame of America's one-party campuses", stated that, "Today's colleges and universities are not, to use the current buzz word, diverse places. Quite the opposite: They are virtual one-party states, ideological monopolies, badly unbalanced ecosystems...They do not, when it comes to political and cultural ideas, look like America."

Leftwing Bias does not just permeate the media and academia, but it also permeates the field of entertainment and the popular culture. The secular leftists are marketing lies to our children in order to lead them away from Judeo-Christian morality. For example, Mel Karmazan's Viacom gives our children Howard Stern, and

Michael Eisner's Disney Corporation's Miramax refused to distribute Mel Gibson's pro-Christ film "The Passion." The Bible states in Isaiah 5:20, "Woe unto them that call evil good, and good evil..." It took a Maverick genius like Mel Gibson to strike a blow for good and against evil in the culture war. He was on his own. The Hollywood establishment would not distribute his film. Instead they mobilized Frank Rich of the *New York Times* in an effort to destroy Mel Gibson and his pro-Christ film. The leftwing elite in Hollywood and New York were stunned when the American people, led by the evangelical Christian "Religious Right," flocked to see Gibson's film in overwhelming numbers. Mel Gibson had inspired Christians to rally around the cross. The secular left has the ability to condone the persecution and the killing of Christians all over the world, but they do not have the ability to kill the faith of dedicated Christians.

Let us now uncover new examples of suppressed history. These examples cover the gamut from modern military history to current events, culture, music, art, ancient history, zoology, anthropology, archeology, geology and religion. But there is a common thread that runs through every one of them. The common thread that binds together all of these seemingly disparate topics is that crucial information concerning them has been suppressed by the liberals in the media and academia, because this crucial information was deemed to be not "politically correct".

This book contains truth that has been censored. Can you handle the truth? If not, don't read this book.

2
Custer's Last Stand

"Custer was our martyr on the altar of Manifest Destiny."
– Professor Paul Andrew Hutton

George Armstrong Custer and his heroic reputation have come under vicious attack recently by the political and academic left. They are doing their best to tear down a traditional American hero who represented the spirit of Manifest Destiny- the idea that America was destined by God to expand from coast to coast, from sea to shining sea.

Custer was considered an American military hero ever since his Civil War exploits starting at Bull Run in 1861, through his defeat of Jeb Stuart's men at Gettysburg in 1863, his participation in the Confederate surrender at Appomattox Court House in 1865, and his defeat of the Indians on the plains at Washita. His heroic last stand at the Little Big Horn in 1876 only served to increase his reputation as an American hero who gave the last full measure of devotion to his country.

Custer, who was killed by Indians in 1876, was still seen as a great American hero up into the 1940's and 1950's. For example, in 1941, Hollywood made a big screen film entitled, *They Died with Their Boots On* staring Errol Flynn as Custer. The swashbuckling leading man Errol Flynn, who is also known for his role as Robin Hood, portrayed Custer very heroically. Custer and the American cavalry were portrayed as the good guys representing Western Civilization. The Indians were portrayed as the bad guys. In 1941, Hollywood was pro-American and America was engaged in WWII.

During the anti-Vietnam War protest era of the late 1960's and early 1970's, the leftwing hippie movement grew in strength, numbers, and influence. Hollywood, the media, and academia turned sharply to the left after the Tet Offensive of 1968. In 1970, in the middle of this leftwing, anti-U.S. military movement, Dustin Hoffman co-starred in a big screen film on Custer entitled, *Little Big Man*. In this film, Custer was portrayed as a crazy, evil villain. The Indians were portrayed as the good guys. It was essentially leftwing agitation propaganda designed to destroy the reputation of a traditional American hero. The political right did not adequately respond to this attack on an American military hero.

In 1991, the leftists who had galvanized and expanded the "political correctness" movement in the 1970's and 1980's, decided to attack again, emboldened by their previous victory over the portrayal of Custer. They pressured the National Park Service to change the name of the "Custer Battlefield National Monument" so that the term "Custer" would not appear in the name of the park. Now that Custer is a villain and not a hero his name must be banned, censored, and purged from the title of the park. The new official, politically correct name for the park is "Little Bighorn Battlefield National Monument". The political right's response to this attack was practically non-existent.

The academic and political left, emboldened by their victories, decided to make a documentary bashing Custer and his men which would air for the first time on the *Discovery Channel* on November 6, 2002. The thesis of this documentary entitled *Unsolved History: Custer's Last Stand*, was that Custer had no last stand. He and his men were cowards who did not put up any tactically organized resistance to the Indian onslaught. They just panicked and were quickly overrun. These leftwing lies, which aired on national television, went virtually unopposed by the political right.

The leftists, emboldened by their string of victories, decided to erect a memorial at the Little Big Horn Battlefield dedicated to the Indians who killed Custer. They did this in June of 2003. Will these leftists try to build a monument dedicated to the Japanese who killed the Americans at Pearl Harbor? Would they put it right next to the Arizona Memorial? This new 2 million dollar memorial dedicated to the Indians who killed Custer was placed on top of the battlefield's ridge so that it will be the last thing people see as they drive away from the park. The political right's response to this attack was practically non-existent.

Why was there no commensurate response by the political right to these leftwing attacks on our culture, on our history, on our heritage, and on our heroes? Why was there no commensurate response by the academic right to these leftwing attacks on our heroes, our heritage, and our history?

The political right was too busy concentrating on current events to be willing or able to delve into an historical event, and the academic right for all intents and purposes does not exist. Leftists dominate the history and political science departments at the universities. There are some conservative intellectual para-academic think tanks in the Washington, D.C. area, but to the best of my knowledge they did not engage in battle over this issue. Apparently, some powerful personae on the political right do not understand the prophetic remarks of George Orwell, that "He who controls the past, controls the future." That is why it is relevant. That is why it must be addressed. This book is an attempt to fill the gap in our cultural battle line through which enemy forces and enemy propaganda is flowing quite freely. We must stanch the tide. We must fill in the gap. We must hold the line.

We must look specifically at the politically correct revisionist history that is being put forth to destroy the reputation of the American hero, George Armstrong Custer. The most highly publicized and disseminated examples of this anti-Custer propaganda were the *Discovery Channel's* "Unsolved History: Custer's Last Stand" and *U.S. News'* "Mysteries of History" special collector's edition p. 31 "Custer's Bluster: His Courageous Last Stand May be a Figment". Both of these works quoted the professor of Anthropology Richard Fox who is the founder of the revisionist theory that there was "no heroic last stand on Custer Hill." It is time to pulverize the sly fox's politically correct paradigm piece-by-piece, point-by-point. It is time for the truth to be revealed. It is time for the anti-hero lies to be exposed.

The *Discovery Channel* documentary, which was based on the research and writings of Richard Fox, started by putting forth the notion that Custer's men in the 7th Cavalry were not elite soldiers in top fighting shape, but were merely young, inexperienced, malnourished, immigrants who were suffering from chronic physical pain. Robert M. Utley refutes this in his book, *Cavalier in Buckskin*, by stating "In the ranks the seventh cavalry was overwhelmingly a veteran regiment. A recent infusion of recruits made up only ten percent of the total. Seventy-five percent claimed one or more years of service, while twenty-seven percent had put in at least one five-year hitch. Twelve men had served fifteen or more years, four twenty, and one twenty-five. The average age was twenty-seven, characteristic of the peacetime army but far higher than in the wartime volunteer outfits." As one can see these men were not, for the most part, inexperienced rookies that didn't know what they were doing.

The documentary implies that Custer was a coward who panicked in combat, had "no tactical organization" and "no heroic last stand". These are outright lies. Custer was a combat veteran of the U.S. Civil War who personally led 21 cavalry charges during the war and had seven horses shot out from under him. He was one who functioned brilliantly in a combat situation. He was not one to panic. The physical evidence at the Little Big Horn Battlefield bears this out. Fox draws conclusions not supported by the evidence.

He does this for political reasons. Custer is considered evil to the leftwing academic elite. They feel his heroic reputation must be destroyed.

Richard Fox did an archeological dig on the Little Big Horn Battlefield in the 1980's. He claims he found spent cartridges distributed upon the battlefield in such a manner as to prove that Custer's men did not put up any stiff resistance to the Indians who overran them that fateful day in 1876. Fox stated, "My research says the outcome was a function of panic and fear. There was no last stand in the gallant, heroic sense." Fox's subjective political conclusions go way beyond his evidentiary findings.

The first major flaw in Fox's not so scientific method is that the battlefield has been picked over and objects removed from it for over one hundred years. Any crime scene investigator knows that first one must secure the crime scene, ensure the chain of custody of any evidence found, bag it, and make sure that people don't have access to rummage through it and contaminate the evidence. Fox is pretending that he can investigate a crime scene after thousands of people have rummaged through it and lifted artifacts for over one hundred years. To say at the outset that there is contamination of the evidence and missing evidence would be an understatement.

Fox claims that he did not find enough cartridges on last stand hill to conclude that Custer put up a valiant fight. The *Discovery Channel* documentary fails to mention that Last Stand Hill was picked over for years and that the first superintendent of the battlefield allowed visitors to keep the "souvenirs" that they found. These "souvenirs" were often spent cartridges from the battle. Last Stand Hill was the favorite place to find spent cartridges, because tourists could leave thinking that maybe they had a spent cartridge fired by Custer during his famous last stand.

The best evidence shows that there was a tactically organized resistance atop Last Stand Hill. That evidence includes the fact that 32 horses were shot and positioned in a semi-circle and as defensive breastworks on Last Stand Hill. Custer and his headquarters' staff were found on the top of the hill. The soldiers' bodies were found in skirmish lines and behind their horse breast works immediately following the battle. The largest group of Indian casualties took place on and around Last Stand Hill. This evidence was gathered immediately following the battle, not one hundred years later. Custer and his men were trying to hold the high ground. This was tactically a smart and organized move. If Reno and Benteen had come to his aid in a timely manner he may have survived. As it was, he was overwhelmed by sheer force of numbers and was slain.

The *Discovery Channel* documentary omitted many Indian eyewitness accounts of intense fighting and organized resistance on Custer Hill. The *Discovery Channel* and Mr. Fox clearly engaged in selective use of evidence. These Indian accounts of hearing fighting on Custer Hill show up in the historical record immediately following the battle. Fox dismisses them and decides to cling to newer more modern

Indian accounts, which downplay Custer's heroism. Sitting Bull himself said that Custer and his soldiers fought bravely (p. 190 *Cavalier in Buckskin*-Utley).

The worst part of the *Discovery Channel* documentary and of Fox's commentary on the Little Big Horn Battle is that Fox draws subjective political conclusions that are not warranted by the objective scientific evidence. It is not just the lack of evidence that is the problem; the problem is also in the faulty interpretation of the existing evidence. Fox may have some expertise in anthropology and political rhetoric, but he seems to lack expertise in military history. For example, Fox says that Custer's men "bunched together" in a "herding instinct" and that proves they were panicked cowards unable to fight. He called it "tactical disintegration". When facing a foe of overwhelming numerical superiority and there is no chance for escape people fight their hardest when their back is "up against the wall." It would not be wise to spread out and get cut off from the main body of your comrades in arms. You would get close to one another, so each man could cover the other man's back. It makes perfect tactical sense in that time and place.

Fox and the *Discovery Channel* documentary also like to use false dichotomies, questions that contain a false premise and straw man arguments. They like to play a political game of semantics in order to tear down an American hero. They try to spin historical evidence to fit their leftwing agenda.

For example, the *Discovery Channel* asks, "Was it a protracted heroic battle or a short devastating route?" Are the two mutually exclusive? Can't there exist a short heroic battle? Most historians believe the battle took about two hours. Sitting Bull's testimony seems to confirm this view. Fox thinks it was 30-45 minutes. Whether it was thirty minutes minimum or the two hours maximum, it doesn't affect at all the heroism or cowardice of the men who fought. The question is based upon a false premise. The documentary goes on to ask, "Did they fight valiantly or were they quickly overrun?" Once again we have a false dichotomy, a false premise, being reiterated to drive home a false point.

Fox concludes emphatically that there was "no heroic last stand on Custer Hill" because he did not find "enough spent cartridges on Last Stand Hill." The *Discovery Channel* concludes its documentary by saying, "It was not a last stand, but a short devastating rout." I have shown their conclusions to be bogus. Their conclusions would be laughable if they weren't so sad. They use these ridiculous lies to impugn the reputation of an American hero. We must take back and successfully defend our history, our heritage, and our heroes.

The secular left wants our children, and all of our descendants to lack any reverence for our God, our country, and our heroes. They want our children and descendants to go adrift like a rudderless ship lost in a sea of humanity. The secular leftists in the media and academia want to destroy the American spirit of Manifest Destiny. They want to destroy Custer because he symbolized the American spirit of Manifest Destiny. The secular leftists are iconoclastic and they consider Custer an icon that must be smashed. In order for the left to discredit the ideal of Manifest Destiny they must first discredit its greatest proponents. The secular left wants to kill our reverence for God, our reverence for country and our reverence for heroes whose purpose was and is to serve our God and country. The left knows that Friedrich Nietzsche was right when he said, "Take away a man's purpose and you've killed the man." In the end, we must be aware that Ayn Rand was right when she said, "Kill reverence, and you've killed the hero in man." As Rick Warren says, to please God is our purpose; if the secular left destroys our purpose then they have destroyed us.

3

Pearl Harbor

"...December 7, 1941, a date which will live in Infamy..."
– President Franklin Delano Roosevelt

The conventional wisdom concerning Franklin Roosevelt and Pearl Harbor is that the attack by Japan had the element of complete surprise. FDR could foresee that Japan would eventually be a threat to the United States because of the way it waged war and its samurai spirit.

FDR was a brilliant President when in his prime. Through the Tennessee Valley Authority, he industrialized the South and brought it back economically to a level with the rest of the country, some seventy years after the Civil War. But before we entered World War II, FDR had a problem. The American people were totally against entering a "foreign war." But if we waited until our own shores were attacked, it might be too late. At this time, only three aircraft carriers and their escorts stood between the United States and defeat by the Japanese in the Pacific.

The conventional wisdom concerning FDR and Pearl Harbor was put forth most exhaustively by Professor Gordon W. Prange in his 800 page tome *At Dawn We Slept* (1981). Professor Donald M. Goldstein and almost all liberal academics followed it from 1941 up to the present day.

Goldstein, who wrote the afterword for Prange's book on Pearl Harbor admitted, "A surprising number of naval personnel interviewed for this study fell into the Roosevelt-planned-it category." Goldstein acted as if he could not understand why any intelligent person would think Roosevelt had foreknowledge of the attack and allowed Pearl Harbor to get hit in order to change public opinion so that he could get into the Second World War. Goldstein wrote, "Such a blood sacrifice was by no means necessary to force the American people to accept entry into the war." Goldstein's assessment is simply not accurate. Prior to the attack on Pearl Harbor, the American population was overwhelmingly isolationist in its foreign policy views. The most popular and powerful Americans at that time (other than President Roosevelt himself) were Henry Ford, Charles Lindbergh and William Randolph Hearst, all of whom were against sending U.S. troops to war in Europe or Asia prior to the Pearl Harbor attack. Like the majority of the U.S. population, they immediately changed their minds with a 180-degree turn after the Japanese attack on Pearl Harbor. The American people did not want to go to war with Spain until the sinking of the *Maine*. The American people did not want to go to war with Germany in WWI until the sinking of the *Lusitania*, and they did not want to go to war with Japan or Germany in WWII until the sinking of the *Arizona*. A former Secretary of the Navy, FD Roosevelt knew his history.

Professor Goldstein, on page 857 of Prange's book *At Dawn We Slept*, in the afterword, inserted that, "Even if one admits Admiral Theobald's assertion that President Roosevelt wanted to have Japan strike first, there would

have been no need to have all the major ships of
the U.S. fleet sit idly in the harbor to be
mercilessly destroyed and many killed." This
statement is simply false. Not "all the major
ships of the U.S. fleet" or even the U.S. Pacific
fleet were in Pearl Harbor on December 7, 1941.
The most important ships, including all aircraft
carriers, were sent out to sea on a fool's errand in
order to save them. Only old obsolete battleships,
which were considered WWI junk, were left
behind as expendable bait. Old battleships like
the *Arizona* were forced to "take one for the team."

These obsolete battleships, the *Arizona,*
Oklahoma, West Virginia, California, Marlyand,
Nevada, Pennsylvania, and *Tennessee* were lined
up like ducks in a shooting gallery to take the full
force of the Japanese naval air arm. It was not
for the men in these ships to "ask or reason why."
It was their mission to fight and die in the highest
tradition as sailors in the United States Navy.
These men and others who were killed at Pearl
Harbor will forever be remembered because of the
Arizona Memorial. No one who understands
history can go aboard the Arizona Memorial
without a great feeling of reverence for these men.

On December 7, 1941, there should have
been three U.S. Aircraft carriers at Pearl Harbor.
But there were none. Where were they? The USS
Saratoga was sent to Puget Sound Navy Yard in
Bremerton, Washington and then on to San
Diego. On November 28, 1941, the USS
Enterprise was ordered to leave Pearl Harbor and
go to Wake Island. On December 5, 1941, the
USS Lexington was sent out of Pearl Harbor to go
to Midway Island on orders from the White

House. (The USS Yorktown was still part of the Atlantic fleet on December 7, 1941.) Conveniently enough there were no U.S. aircraft carriers in Pearl Harbor on December 7, 1941. When U.S. and Japanese ships fought at Midway, none of them could see the enemy ships from the decks of their own ships. For all the fighting took place at great distances because of the lethality and range of aircraft launched from the decks of the carriers. All naval planners knew that in an era of carriers, battleships were strategically obsolete.

Admiral Bloch testified to Congress that, "The Japanese only destroyed a lot of old hardware. In a sense they did us a favor." On December 7, 1941 at 2:15 p.m., after hearing the initial news of the attack on Pearl Harbor, FDR told Lord Halifax, "Most of the fleet was at sea...none of their newer ships were in harbor."

Robert B. Stinnett wrote in his book *Day of Deceit: The Truth About FDR and Pearl Harbor* that, "On orders from Washington, Kimmel left his oldest vessels inside Pearl Harbor and sent twenty-one modern warships, including his two aircraft carriers, west toward Wake and Midway. With the departure of the *Lexington* and *Enterprise* groups, the warships remaining in Pearl Harbor were mostly 27 year old relics of World War I."

Let us step back and look at why Japan attacked the United States on December 7, 1941. President Roosevelt desperately wanted to get into WWII so that he could help the British and later the Russians destroy Nazi Germany. The problem was that an overwhelming majority of the American people, as shown in opinion polls at that time, did not want to go to war in Europe again. The bloody trenches of WWI were promised by Woodrow Wilson to be "the war to end all wars." Americans had drifted back to the George Washington thesis of "beware of foreign entanglements." Hearst who was a media mogul, Charles Lindbergh who was a world famous celebrity and American aviation hero, and Henry Ford who was the first person to mass produce affordable automobiles, were all against U.S. involvement in WWII prior to December 7, 1941. Japan was on the move in Asia and had taken over a good part of the coast of China. FDR saw an opportunity, which has been called the "back door to war". FDR would provoke Japan to attack America so that he could go to war with the full support of the American people.

FDR's plan to provoke Japan into attacking the United States was formally written up into an eight-point memo by Lieutenant Commander Arthur H. McCollum, head of the Far East desk of The Office of Naval Intelligence (ONI). This 8-point memo was dated October 7, 1940. It reads as follows:

1.) Make an arrangement with Britain for the use of British bases in the Pacific, particularly Singapore.
2.) Make an arrangement with Holland for the use of base facilities and acquisition of supplies in the Dutch East Indies.
3.) Give all possible aid to the Chinese government of Chiang Kai-Shek.

4.) Send a division of long-range heavy cruisers to the Orient, Philippines, or Singapore.

5.) Send two divisions of submarines to the Orient.

6.) Keep the main strength of the U.S. fleet, now in the Pacific, in the vicinity of the Hawaiian Islands.

7.) Insist that the Dutch refuse to grant Japanese demands for undue economic concessions, particularly oil.

8.) Completely embargo all trade with Japan, in collaboration with a similar embargo imposed by the British Empire.

The most important point in this memo, which FDR put into practice, was the embargo on all trade with Japan, which included cutting off Japan's oil supplies. Japan's home islands lack the natural resources of oil, and therefore, they must get their oil from foreigners. Oil is the lifeblood of a modern industrialized state. Cutting off Japan's oil supply is like cutting off a man's oxygen intake. Soon he will die. So he is forced to fight off the attacker who has his hands around his throat.

The preeminent British military historian Captain B.H. Liddell Hart wrote in his book, *History of the Second World War*, "President Roosevelt issued orders on the 26th of July, 1941 freezing all Japanese assets in the United States and placing an embargo on oil supply. Mr. Churchill took simultaneous action, and two days later the refugee Dutch Government in London was induced to follow suit, which meant, as Churchill had remarked, 'Japan was deprived at a stroke of her vital oil supplies'."

Liddell Hart went on to write, "In earlier discussions, as far back as 1931, it had always been recognized that such a paralyzing stroke would force Japan to fight, as the only alternative to collapse or the abandonment of her policy. It is remarkable that she deferred striking for more than four months, while trying to negotiate a lifting of the oil embargo. The United States Government refused to lift it unless Japan withdrew not only from Indo-China, but also from China. No government, least of all the Japanese, could be expected to swallow such humiliating conditions, and such 'loss of face'. So there was every reason to expect war in the Pacific at any moment, from the last week of July onwards. In these circumstances the Americans and British were lucky to be allowed four months' grace before the Japanese struck. But little advantage was taken of this interval for defensive preparation."

The military historian John Keegan, in his book *The Price of Admiralty*, wrote that President Roosevelt's 26 July 1941 order forbidding the export of oil to Japan denied Japan of 80% of her oil imports. Keegan wrote, "The urgency was imposed by the oil embargo, which diminished reserves at a million barrels a month. By September the country (whose domestic production was but 400,000 tons against an annual consumption of 12 million tons) had only a little over a year's supply left and was approaching a threshold minimum it could not afford to cross."

The Japanese were not just provoked verbally or psychologically, but they felt they were provoked physically when FDR started choking off their oil supply. The die had been cast. They had to fight. They now turned to their most brilliant military mind and naval strategist Admiral Yamamoto.

Admiral Yamamoto gave an important and dramatic speech to the Japanese high command in the summer of 1941. Before Yamamoto spoke, other Japanese officers floated their plans for war in the Pacific. These plans were often piecemeal and tried to avoid the "elephant in the living room," The United States of America. Yamamoto disagreed with these plans. Everyone awaited with baited breath the plan to be put forth by the well-traveled and highly educated Admiral Yamamoto.

When Yamamoto ascended the podium, the room fell silent. Yamamoto started his speech by reiterating Colonel Iwakuro Hideo's warnings from the Japanese army-navy conference of August 1941. He warned them about America's superior industrial might compared to Japan's. America's superiority over Japan in steel production is 20:1; in coal, 10:1; aircraft, 5:1; labor, 5:1; shipping, 2:1; oil, 100:1. "Overall he estimated the war potential of the United States was ten times greater than that of Japan."

Yamamoto paused to let the statistics sink in to his audience. He then said, "In the face of such odds, I can see little hope of success in any ordinary strategy." He ended every paragraph of his speech with the refrain, "Japan can not defeat the United States by any ordinary strategy." His refrain begged the question. His audience asked him the question after he seemingly concluded his remarks with the pregnant phrase, "Japan can not defeat the United States by any ordinary strategy." "Then by what extraordinary strategy can we use to defeat the United States?" Yamamoto then proceeded to lay out his plans for the Pearl Harbor attack.

The goal of the Pearl Harbor attack was to knock out the U.S. Pacific fleet in one huge surprise attack. To use a boxing analogy, America had much better endurance, was better conditioned, and was in superior shape. If the fight went more than three rounds America would win. Time was on America's side. The Japanese boxer's only chance of success in this fight would be to knock out the American fighter with a sucker punch before the bell sounded to start the first round. In that case conditioning does not matter. Japan had the aircraft carrier strength to deliver this knockout blow. Japan had a brilliant plan, which depended on the element of surprise to execute this knockout blow. What the Japanese did not realize was that the United States had broken both the Japanese diplomatic code and the Japanese naval code. The Japanese would not have the element of surprise they so desperately needed, and they would not have the opportunity at Pearl Harbor to destroy America's aircraft carriers. Shortly before the attack they would be sent away for safekeeping. When Admiral Yamamoto received word back from the Pearl Harbor attack indicating that none of the

U.S. Aircraft carriers were sunk, he became depressed and issued his famous quotation, "I am afraid that we have awakened a sleeping giant."

In 1982, John Toland's book, *Infamy*, was published. It was the first major book in many years to come out and say that FDR knew about the impending attack on Pearl Harbor "but remained silent so that the U.S. would be drawn into the war." Toland who is considered to be one of the best World War II historians in the world, interviewed "Seaman Z" or Robert Ogg, a first hand witness to American foreknowledge of the Pearl Harbor attack, who had never been interviewed before by any historian, nor had he ever been called to testify in any Congressional hearing or investigation into the Pearl Harbor affair. Toland's new research shed new light on the Pearl Harbor attack.

In the year 2000, Robert Stinnett in his book, *Day of Deceit: The Truth About FDR and Pearl Harbor*, confirmed the veracity of Toland's thesis and of Ogg's testimony. Stinnett wrote, "In his book *Infamy*, published in 1982, John Toland wrote that San Francisco's Twelfth Naval District obtained radio direction finder bearing that placed Japanese warships in the Pacific Ocean north of Hawaii from about November 30 to December 4, 1941. Toland's source was Robert Ogg, who in 1941, was on the staff of the Naval District Intelligence Office as a special investigator. Ogg stated that verification of his account could be found in Dutch Harbor, [Alaska] records. Today, over fifty years later, those records have been found. Captain Richard McCullough, the District's Intelligence Chief, told

Ogg that he forwarded the alert over a secure radio circuit to Washington, where the information reached the White House." In October of 1985, Stinnett discovered the 4000-kilocycle Dutch Harbor reports referred to by Ogg. Stinnett reported in his book published in 2000 that, "They irrefutably confirm Ogg's intercept details."

Toland wrote that General George C. Marshall, head of the Army, and Admiral Harold Stark, head of the Navy, sent to their commanders on November 27, 1941, orders that stated, "The United States desires that Japan commit the first overt act period."

When the U.S. government broke the "purple code"-the Japanese diplomatic code-The White House did not tell Kimmell or Short about it. Kimmel and Short were the two U.S. Commanders in Pearl Harbor, Hawaii. Toland went on to say that Naval Intelligence decoded the "winds" execute message on December 4, 1941. It read "Higashi no kaze ame." "East wind, rain." It meant that war with a nation to the east of Japan-The United States- was about to commence. This decoded message was sent to the White House, but it was never passed on to Kimmell or Short.

Robert Stinnett utilized the Freedom of Information Act to get access to documents on Pearl Harbor that had never been seen before by scholars or by the general public. This new information convinced him that FDR knew about the impending attack on Pearl Harbor, but that he wanted to take the hit so he could get into WWII with total approval from Congress and the

American people. Secretary of War Henry
Stimson wrote in his diary, "In spite of the risk
involved, however, in letting the Japanese fire the
first shot, we realized that in order to have the full
support of the American people, it was desirable
to make sure the Japanese be the ones to do this,
so that there should remain no doubt in anyone's
mind as to who were the aggressors." Stinnett
wrote that, "Conclusive cryptographic evidence
indicates that FDR left the Pacific fleet [at Pearl
Harbor] in harms way." Stinnett also proves with
his new evidence that the Japanese broke radio
silence.
   CAST reports from Corregidor, TESTM
records obtained by Stinnett through the
Freedom of Information Act in 1986, and code
breaker Navy Captain Duane Whitlock, confirmed
the fact that the Japanese did not have total
"radio silence."
   The United States did not just break the
Japanese Diplomatic Code (Purple) prior to
December 7, 1941, but the U.S. also broke the
Japanese Naval Code prior to December 7, 1941.
Stinnett wrote, "By November 16, 1941,
Lankford's colleagues at CAST reported another
monumental breakthrough: They had solved the
main operational code of the Japanese Navy. The
commanding officer of CAST, Lieutenant John M.
Lietwiler, wrote Washington that his staff had
succeeded in intercepting, decoding, and
translating the Japanese Naval Operations code:
'We are reading enough current traffic to keep two
translators very busy.' Lietwiler's admission that
his cryptographers had broken the prime
Japanese Naval Code has been kept in secret U.S.

Navy vaults until the May 2000 Freedom of Information Act release. It was not listed in the U.S. Navy index accompanying the records nor in the index prepared by Archives II."

Stinnett concluded the afterword to the paperback edition of *Day of Deceit* by stating, "Overwhelming evidence contained in the May 2000 Freedom of Information Act release, reveals that by mid-November 1941, as Japanese naval forces headed for Hawaii, America's radio cryptographers had solved the principal Japanese Naval Codes and that Japan's top Admirals went on the Japanese Naval airways and in a series of radio messages disclosed that Pearl Harbor was the target of their raid."

President FDR had both the Japanese Diplomatic Code and the Japanese Naval Code broken by November 16, 1941. This gave FDR the time he needed to order the two remaining U.S. Aircraft Carriers stationed at Pearl Harbor out to sea. He sent the Enterprise out of harms way on November 28, 1941, and he sent the Lexington out of harms way on December 5, 1941.

All historians admit that the American knowledge of the Japanese Naval Code, often referred to as JN-25, was one of the crucial factors in the American naval victory over the Japanese at Midway, six months after the Pearl Harbor attack. At the Battle of Midway, the U.S. could concentrate its naval forces and sink four Japanese aircraft carriers; partially because of the fact it knew every move Japan was going to make before they made it. They knew this because of the broken code.

In boxing terminology, FDR was merely playing rope-a-dope. FDR at Pearl Harbor put himself on the ropes and covered his head with his gloves. He allowed the Japanese to waste their energy punching his forearms, which covered his face. Later in the fight FDR came off the ropes, fresh as could be and decimated the Japanese with four knockout blows before the Japanese could even hit the canvas. Midway was the turning point in this international boxing match.

FDR died before Japan was willing to surrender. President Truman won the war with Japan. Hiroshima and Nagasaki were the final rounds of the match, which forced Japan to surrender unconditionally.

Most of the evidence concerning the fact that the United States had broken the Japanese Naval Code prior to Pearl Harbor was suppressed from 1941 up until the year 2000. Stinnett estimates that the U.S. Navy is still suppressing approximately 143,000 Japanese naval intercepts on grounds of national security. At least enough information has been released so that we now know the gist of the truth. FDR knew.

4
The Bay of Pigs

"We are under attack by two sea fury aircraft and heavy artillery. Do not see friendly air cover as you promised. Need Jet support immediately! This is Cuba calling. Where will help come from? This is Cuba calling the free world. We need help in Cuba...send all available aircraft now! Out of ammunition. Enemy closing in. Help must arrive in next hour...can't wait any longer. Destroying my radio now."
– Francisco "Pepe" Hernandez (Anti-Castro Cuban pleading for help at the Bay of Pigs in April of 1961.)

Why did American backed anti-communist Cubans fail to overthrow the fledgling government of Fidel Castro in April of 1961? The anti-Castro Cubans of Brigade 2506 tried valiantly but to no avail. Their attempted liberation of Cuba is now known to history as the Bay of Pigs Invasion. Why did the Bay of Pigs invasion fail?

Most American History textbooks are written by leftwing professors. As a result of this fact, most U.S. History textbooks say the Bay of Pigs invasion failed because the CIA underestimated Castro's popularity. This prevented the mass uprising of the populace against Castro as predicted by the CIA once Brigade 2506 invaded Cuba. In short the leftwing professors say "the CIA bungled it, and President John F. Kennedy did nothing wrong except for trusting the CIA's advice. End of story."

The truth as to why the Bay of Pigs Invasion failed is suppressed from most U.S. History textbooks. It is my goal here to bring forth that suppressed truth, and to lay bare the facts as to why the Bay of Pigs Invasion failed. The Bay of Pigs invasion failed because President John F. Kennedy made two horrible decisions.

First, Kennedy made the fateful decision to change the invasion-landing site at the last hour. The original invasion plan, supported by President Eisenhower, Richard Bissel, and Charles Cabell of the CIA was to land the invasion force on the beaches of Trinidad, Cuba.

They picked Trinidad, Cuba for three reasons. First, it had a large population of Cuban people who were strongly opposed to the Castro regime. These people could be armed with the huge cache of extra rifles and ammunition from Brigade 2506 supply ships once they were successfully unloaded onto the beach. This would lead to a rapid and immediate swelling of the size of the anti-Castro military force within Cuba. Second, they picked Trinidad, Cuba because it bordered the Escambry Mountain Range, which would allow for the implementation of the contingency plan of going into the mountains in order to wage an organized guerilla campaign against the Castro government, if Castro's government did not collapse early on in the fighting. This would merely turn the tables on Castro, because Castro waged a similar guerilla campaign against Batista (The former Cuban Head of State) from the Sierra Maestre Mountains. History proves it could be done. Third, Trinidad, Cuba also had an airstrip to fly in supplies, and from which to launch missions. It was the perfect landing spot according to former President and General Dwight Eisenhower, Director of the CIA Dulles, and Deputy Director of Plans Bissell.

President Kennedy was scared. He did not want the Soviet Union to find out that the United States was militarily supporting the Cuban exiles invasion of Cuba in 1961. Kennedy wanted U.S. assistance completely covert. He did not want a big U.S. footprint on the operation. He wanted the U.S. to keep a low profile. Concerning U.S. involvement, he wanted to maintain "plausible deniability." As a result of these facts, Kennedy ordered the invasion plans to be changed from Trinidad, Cuba, where Kennedy thought there were too many people and it would cause a big stir, to the Cochinos Bay, i.e. the Bay of Pigs, which was a sparsely populated swampy area, which would produce a lower profile.

This decision by Kennedy to change the invasion site greatly reduced the chances and feasibility of a mass armed uprising against Castro's government.

The second horrible decision President Kennedy made, which doomed the Bay of Pigs invasion to failure, was his decision to cancel crucial air-strikes at literally the last minute. In modern day sports terminology this is known as "a game day decision." The problem is no one else on the team knew it was "a game day decision." The CIA plan originally approved by Eisenhower and later approved by Kennedy, who gave the green light on it, called for a series of U.S. air strikes to destroy all of Castro's air force, which contained a grand total of only two jets and a few other WWII era propeller driven airplanes. The CIA and the U.S. military told Kennedy it was crucial to the success of the plan for total "air superiority", "air cover", an "air umbrella", to protect the invasion forces and its ships. For without adequate air cover the invasion would surely fail.

The Cuban exiles of Brigade 2506 had no ability to shoot down or defend against Castro's small air force. They were only willing to invade Cuba if America promised to give them total air cover and to destroy Castro's air force on the ground and in the air. President Kennedy agreed to this plan. At the last minute, he changed his mind. He cancelled the crucial air strikes.

Castro's two jets strafed the Cuban exile invaders, killing many of them. Castro's two jets shot down the Cuban exiles' only propeller driven planes. Castro's two jets sunk the invasion forces' supply ships, which carried trucks, tanks, the rifles, and ammunition, which had the potential to arm the populace of Cuba in a mass uprising against the Communist government. These supply ships were also crucial for the invading force itself. Without them, they were not going to last more than a few days.

All this took place while American naval aviators were suited up and ready to go in their cockpits on the flat top surface of an American aircraft carrier right off the Cuban shore. At the last minute President Kennedy ordered them to abort their planned on and promised mission. This fateful decision doomed the invaders. It was a stab in the back, a betrayal of great magnitude.

It is remembered on Ocho Street in Miami, Florida to this day. "...Every year on April 17, at one minute past midnight, the honor guard of the Bay of Pigs Brigade begins a vigil before their 'monument of heroes' at 13th Avenue and Calle Ocho (Eighth Street) in the heart of Little Havana in Miami. President of the Brigade Juan Perez Franco reads the names of each of the 100-some Cuban freedom fighters that died in combat on land, at sea and in the air. As each name is called, the veterans, family and friends respond, 'Presente!' Present!"

It is why the first wave of Cubans to settle in Miami, the ones who fled from Castro's dictatorship in the 1960's, vote solidly Republican to this day. They are anti-Communist because they know first hand what Communism is all about. They do not vote for Democrats, because Kennedy proved to them that Democrats at the national level are soft on Communism.

The Bay of Pigs invasion failed because Kennedy changed the landing site and called off crucial air strikes at the last minute. The Bay of Pigs invasion failed because President Kennedy failed. These facts do not cease to be facts merely because leftwing professors omit them from their works.

How did the key American players in the Bay of Pigs invasion feel about President Kennedy's decision to cancel promised U.S. air strikes at the last minute?

"When the Deputy Director of the CIA, General Charles P. Cabell, was given the order to cancel the air strike, he felt he had been hit by a 'falling bomb'. He was an expert on air support.

He had worked on plans for the Normandy invasion. It was clear to Cabell that the promised protection of the Brigade from the air was vital" (Wyden, 1979).

The two top CIA men, Bissell and Cabell, and the top navy man Admiral Burke, pleaded with Kennedy to reinstate the air cover. Kennedy refused. The anti-Castro Cubans who went ashore did not know that their air support had been cancelled until it was too late. According to Jack Skelly in his article entitled, *Ducking the Blame at the Bay of Pigs*, "the invasion began at 1 a.m. with the first troops going ashore at the Bay of Pigs and six planes of Castro's air force surviving. Two T-33 jet trainers with rockets and 50-caliber machine guns sank the invasion ships and downed the slow B-26's over the Bay of Pigs. When the freedom fighters ran out of ammunition on the third day, they had to surrender or die."

One of the anti-Castro Cuban leaders said, "Pulling out the rug at the last minute like that is absolutely reprehensible, no it's criminal!" (Wyden, 1979.)

The CIA's former chief historian, Jack Pfeiffer, wrote, "President Kennedy cancelled crucial air strikes. It was this decision that doomed the operation from the start" (Peterzell, 1987).

To what extent do history books written by leftwing American intellectuals censor the truth concerning the Bay of Pigs?

Most U.S. history textbook authors are leftist/liberal Democrats who worship the ground upon which President Kennedy walked. As a result of this fact, many U.S. history textbooks either omit the fact that Kennedy cancelled the promised U.S. air strikes at the Bay of Pigs or they mention it and say that even with those air strikes the invasion would have failed, because there was no popular uprising as predicted by the CIA. The leftist spin-doctors shift the blame for the failure at the Bay of Pigs from Kennedy to the CIA.

This leftwing spin was first put forward by Kennedy's own political advisers and liberal journalist friends immediately following the Bay of Pigs fiasco. Jack Skelly reports in his article entitled, *Ducking the Blame at the Bay of Pigs*, that "...on the fourth day of the invasion, when it was obvious that the operation had failed, Kennedy accepted blame for the disaster in an address to the American Association of Newspaper Editors. He then sent his spin doctors to lunch at expensive Washington restaurants with influential columnists, radio commentators and TV reporters to make sure the word got out that those to blame were a bumbling CIA, an incompetent Joint Chiefs of Staff- and the poorly trained and lightly armed Cubans. JFK was quoted to the favored journalists, (off the record, of course), as saying, ' How could I have been so stupid' to trust such a gang?" This leftwing spin, which blames the CIA and makes Kennedy smell like a rose can be found in Arthur Schlessinger's book *A Thousand Days: John F. Kennedy in the White House*, Ted Sorensen's book *Kennedy*, and Haynes Johnson's book *The Bay of Pigs: The Leader's Story of Brigade 2506*. In order for these three books to successfully promote their leftwing propaganda, they had to suppress crucial facts concerning the Bay of Pigs. As Grayston L. Lynch wrote, "not one of the three provides even one word about how many air strikes were proposed and cancelled by the new frontier [Kennedy Administration] because of State Department objections. Nor do they mention that five strikes of sixteen planes each- strikes at first light on Saturday, Sunday, and Monday and last-light strikes on Saturday and Sunday- were approved by President Kennedy at the final full-scale meeting on April 4."

Grayston L. Lynch went on to write that Castro's total air force at the time consisted of only "two T-33 jets, three sea furies, and two B-26 bombers. All of the brigade 2506 planes were shot down by the two Castro T-33 jets. The cancellation of the only remaining air strike against Castro's jets, a cancellation that doomed the 2506 Brigade, cost the lives of many good men, and one year later was to bring the world to the brink of nuclear war."

Many Leftists in American academia claim that Kennedy's cancellation of the air strikes at the Bay of Pigs is a moot point because the invasion would have failed anyway due to their small number (1,400) and due to the fact that this number never increased through the CIA's predicted mass uprising of the Cuban populace.

As far as the popular uprising argument goes, most people usually wait to see which side is going to win and then they jump in on the winning side, in order to gain the spoils of victory and to avoid the bitter taste of imprisonment or execution for having joined the losing side in an attempted coup d'etat. There was no popular uprising for two reasons. First, President Kennedy changed the location for the invasion of Cuba from a highly populous area to an isolated sparsely populated area, where there was no place to hide to conduct guerilla operations. Second, President Kennedy cancelled the air strikes which allowed Castro's two jets to win a decisive military victory including the sinking of the brigades' supply ships; the very ships that held vital guns and ammo, which were crucial for the operation's success.

No one wants to jump on to help a losing cause that will force your family into prison or in front of an execution squad. If it looked like the anti-Castro Cuban forces were going to win because all of Castro's air force had been wiped out and the pro-American forces had total air superiority, then more people would have jumped on the winning band-wagon and Castro would have been ousted from power in 1961, just like a small band of CIA trained exiles overthrew the government of Guatemala in 1954 with U.S. air-cover. It took less than a week. Instead, Castro would outlive Eisenhower, Kennedy, Johnson, Nixon, and Reagan.

The members of Brigade 2506 are combat heroes whose kill ratios in battle were quite impressive. Grayston L. Lynch wrote that they were "outnumbered in every battle by at least twenty to one, and had inflicted heavy casualties on Castro's forces, at a rate of more than fifty to one."

Grayston L. Lynch knows of what he speaks. He is a retired U.S. Army Captain and former CIA officer. He was wounded at

Normandy, in the Battle of the Bulge, and
Heartbreak Ridge in Korea; served with special
forces in Laos, and received 3 purple hearts, two
silver stars, and one bronze star with a V for
valor. He joined the CIA in 1960. For his
heroism at the Bay of Pigs, Lynch was awarded
the Intelligence Star, the CIA's most coveted
award.

    In some leftwing intellectual circles it is
popular to blame "group-think" for the failure at
the Bay of Pigs. This theory is clearly bogus;
Peter Wyden impressively debunked it in his book
on the Bay of Pigs.

> "But too much can be made of
> group dynamics. The five key
> decisions of the Bay of Pigs were not
> made in a group, nor even, for the
> most part, in a group setting: (1) The
> decision to escalate the adventure
> from a plausibly deniable infiltration
> effort into an invasion was made in
> Bissell's head; (2) the decision to
> weaken the first air strike and make
> it "minimal" was made unilaterally
> by Kennedy; (3) the decision to
> cancel the second strike was made
> by Kennedy late on a Sunday night
> by phone in consultation with Rusk
> and Bundy; (4) the decision to give
> the "go" order was made by Kennedy
> after extensive lonely soul-
> searching; (5) the decision not to
> escalate the invasion in the face of
> great temptation posed by incipient

> disaster- to become a "bum," not an
> aggressor- was made by the
> President, sparring fiercely with
> Admiral Burke; other advisers were
> practically silent."

The blame for the failure at the Bay of Pigs lies clearly on John F. Kennedy's doorstep.

Grayston Lynch, who participated first hand in the Bay of Pigs invasion, was told to testify to the U.S. government as to what happened and what went wrong. He did so, but Bobby Kennedy suppressed key portions of his testimony. According to Lynch, the following portion of his testimony was suppressed/omitted from the transcripts and final reports of the hearings. It disappeared because it was not "politically correct" although it was factually correct.

> "I felt very strongly that the
> Cochinos Plan had been sound and
> had been successful up to the time
> of the first Castro air attack. From
> that point onward, many things
> went wrong, none of which would
> have happened had the Castro
> planes been destroyed on the
> ground, as planned."

Bobby Kennedy felt the need to suppress first hand history from a hero.

President Kennedy wanted to pacify and protect the reputation and credibility of his ambassador to the United Nations Adlai Stevenson. Stevenson was claiming at the U.N.

the U.S. had no involvement in the Bay of Pigs invasion. The other delegates at the U.N. were having trouble buying his story. Adlai Stevenson and Dean Rusk, two of the most liberal advisers in Kennedy's cabinet, successfully lobbied President Kennedy to cancel the planned U.S. air strikes in support of the Bay of Pigs operation in order to maintain what they perceived to be some level of credibility at the U.N. They argued that if a U.S. pilot was shot down over Cuba, they would be seen as liars and the U.S.'s "plausible deniability" would no longer be plausible. Kennedy, Rusk, and Stevenson felt it was more important to curry favor with the United Nations than to support a friend in need. Leftists love the U.N., but they hate anti-communist freedom fighters. Kennedy, Rusk, and Stevenson believed in the U.N. but not Brigade 2506.

Why didn't President Kennedy call off the Bay of Pigs invasion before it started? President Kennedy knew that the plan for Cuban exiles to invade Cuba and oust Castro could not succeed without help from the United States. He knew that he did not want to give the Cuban exiles the help they needed to secure victory. So why did Kennedy allow the invasion to go forward? Why didn't President Kennedy just cancel the invasion altogether instead of giving the green light to the invasion and then cutting off their air support at the last minute after the attack had commenced?

I found a rather shocking answer to this question. The most provocative quotation I found concerning the Bay of Pigs invasion was issued by Grayston Lynch on page 81 of his book *Decision for Disaster: Betrayal at the Bay of Pigs*. Lynch wrote, "Kennedy did not send the Brigade to Cuba to get rid of Castro. He sent it to Cochinos Bay to get rid of those men." [He sent it to get rid of Brigade 2506.]

When I first read that quotation by Lynch, I thought it might be hyperbole. I thought maybe he was making a slight exaggeration for poetic effect. But as I did further research for this chapter on the Bay of Pigs, I realized that Lynch's provocative quote might not be hyperbole, but that it may be literal truth. For on page 100 of Peter Wyden's book *Bay of Pigs: The Untold Story*, it states, "Dulles sounded a note of urgency. 'Don't forget that we have a disposal problem' he said. 'If we have to take these men out of Guatemala, we will have to transfer them to the United States, and we can't have them wandering around the country telling everyone what they have been doing.' Demobilization in Guatemala would be worse. The Cubans might resist being disarmed. If they were successfully dispersed they would spread word all over Latin America of how the United States turned tail. This could trigger Communist takeovers elsewhere in the hemisphere. Without enthusiasm, the president agreed it might be best to let the exiles go to the destination of their choice: Cuba. To avoid anti-American reaction in the United Nations, he wanted American sponsorship thoroughly concealed."

One cannot read minds, but based on the evidence the following scenario is plausible:

President Kennedy did not cancel the Bay of Pigs invasion because he believed that if he did cancel it, it would leave him with a "disposal

problem". He would have angry armed Cuban
exiles running around Miami, Florida all dressed
up with no place to go. Kennedy thought they
would pose a political if not physical threat to his
government. He felt that he needed to dispose of
them. Sending them to Cuba and canceling their
U.S. air support at the last minute would kill two
birds with one stone. He may have thought it
would kill Brigade 2506 and that it would
maintain his and Stevenson's contention that the
U.S. was not involved. In the end it turned out
quite differently. Many of the members of Brigade
2506 outlived President Kennedy, and U.S.
involvement in the operation was essentially an
open secret.

Today, the anti-Castro Cubans of Brigade
2506 and their descendants wield considerable
power in Miami, Florida. They were insulted once
again by a liberal Democrat by the name of Bill
Clinton, when he forced at gun point Elian
Gonzalez back to Castro's Communist Cuba after
his mother sacrificed her life to get her son out of
Cuba and into the United States. Because of the
Bay of Pigs and its handling by President
Kennedy, the anti-Castro Cuban community in
Miami, Florida is one of the most patriotic, pro-
American, pro-Republican Party groups in the
United States.

I ended my most recent lecture to high
school students concerning the Bay of Pigs with a
piece of advice: If you ever date an upper-class
Cuban American girl in Miami, Florida, and she
invites you to dinner at her parents' house, and
her parents ask you, "Who is your favorite
president of the United States?" Don't answer by

saying, "President John F. Kennedy"; for if you do, you will probably never be allowed to see that girl again.

5
The Tet Offensive-Vietnam 1968

"When I lost Walter, I lost the war."
– President Lyndon B. Johnson

In the latter part of the Civil War, Robert E. Lee fought three brilliant defensive battles when Grant invaded the South. In these battles, known as the Wilderness, Spotsylvania, and Cold Harbor, the Union lost 63,000 men – more men than Lee had in his entire army.

Grant and Lincoln knew they could, numerically speaking, replace their losses, so they decided to press on in spite of the inordinate number of casualties they had suffered. But what if all these dead men were shown on television every night at 6:30? The North would have sued for peace, given up, cut and run, and we would be two separate nations today: The U.S.A. in the north and the C.S.A. in the south.

A similar scenario played out during the Vietnam War. During the Vietnam War parts of the war, especially the Tet Offensive of 1968, were on television news broadcasts every night at 6:30. One of the most important battles of The Tet Offensive was the battle of Khe Sanh. Hardly anyone in the U.S. knew why the U.S. Marines were at Khe Sanh in the first place, not even the people who watched the news every night at 6:30.

The news media had the U.S. public believe the marines at Khe Sanh were dying for nothing, even though the Marines wiped out the two elite North Vietnamese divisions that had assaulted and destroyed the French at Dien Bien Phu.

General Giap and his North Vietnamese
Communist Divisions were hoping for another
Dien Bien Phu. But there would be no deja vu.
For fighting a small group of abandoned
Frenchmen who had no air support is one thing,
but fighting the U.S. Marines who had total air
superiority is entirely another thing.

The U.S. Marines won decisively at Khe
Sanh. They held on to their base. The Marines
lost 205 men. The North Vietnamese
Communists in the siege of Khe Sanh, which
lasted from January 21st to April 7, 1968, lost
10,000 men. But the U.S. lost in Washington
D.C. Lyndon B. Johnson lost support of the U.S.
public and gave up his plans to interdict the Ho
Chi Minh Trail with U.S. ground forces. The U.S.
Marines were ordered to abandon Khe Sanh in
June of 1968.

The Communist Tet Offensive of 1968 was a
huge military victory for the U.S. armed forces,
but the U.S. news media blatantly lied and said
just the opposite every night at 6:30. They said
that the U.S. armed forces were completely
surprised and defeated in Khe Sanh, Hue, and
Saigon. The leftists in the U.S. news media
painted a false picture of Communist invincibility.
The American people lost all hope for victory.

After the Tet Offensive, Walter Cronkite,
who was then the CBS evening news anchorman,
turned even more against the prosecution of the
war in Vietnam. He could not stand American
military victory over Communism. So he lied and
reported that the U.S. military was defeated in the
Tet Offensive. Walter Cronkite, after Tet, went on
national television to advocate that the U.S.

should cut and run and abandon South Vietnam to the Communists. Cronkite said, "The only rational way out...would be to negotiate, not as victors." President Lyndon B. Johnson summed it all up when he said, "When I lost Walter, I lost the war."

Now let us look at some more details concerning the Tet Offensive and its aftermath. Another major battle in the Tet Offensive was the battle for Hue, the old imperial capital of Vietnam. The Communists took over its Citadel and the city during the initial phase of the Tet offensive. American Marines retook the Citadel and the city in less than a month. 147 American Marines were killed at Hue. 5,113 Communist troops were killed at Hue. As Victor Davis Hanson said, "Hue was yet another impressive American military victory."

Leftists in the U.S. news media enjoyed most the Communist's attack on the American embassy in Saigon during the Tet Offensive in Vietnam in 1968. Leftwing journalists falsely reported that the Viet Cong had taken over the American embassy and were in control of the main chancery. The truth was that within five hours every Communist on the embassy grounds was killed. The U.S. was in total control of its embassy.

Besides Walter Cronkite, who were some of the other American traitors who wanted the communists to take over Vietnam? Jane Fonda and Tom Hayden named their son Troi after a Vietnamese Communist warrior. David Halberstam wrote a biography of Ho Chi Minh, portraying the communist dictator of North

Vietnam in a glowing positive light. One of Halberstam's main sources for his book on Ho Chi Minh was Jean Lacouture's account of Ho Chi Minh. Lacouture was a French leftist who later admitted that his writings on Ho Chi Minh were essentially pieces of Communist propaganda, which omitted Ho Chi Minh's flaws and omitted the flaws and atrocities of his Communist regime.

During the Tet Offensive, in Saigon in 1968, a Viet Cong infiltrator broke into the home of a South Vietnamese army officer who served under the ARVN General, Nguyen Ngoc Loan (ARVN was the South Vietnamese military, which was allied with the Americans). This communist Viet Cong thug murdered the South Vietnamese officer, his wife, and their children while they were in bed. As the good guys were fighting for their lives against the Viet Cong infiltrators, General Nguyen Ngoc Loan personally executed the captured Viet Cong infiltrator that had just killed many of his men. An associated press photographer, Eddie Adams, won a Pulitzer Prize for photography because of his photograph of this execution in the streets of Saigon. This picture of a South Vietnamese General using his pistol to blow the brains out of a man with his hands tied behind his back was used by the leftists in the U.S. news media as a propaganda piece to help the Communist cause. It was to make the U.S. and their South Vietnamese allies look like the bad guys. No context was given. No mention was made of the fact that the man who was executed was a Communist criminal who murdered little children in bed. The intentional omission of these pertinent facts symbolizes the leftwing bias in the American media.

The most memorable quotation from the Tet Offensive may actually be a hoax perpetrated by a leftwing journalist in order to help out the Communist cause. In his Book *Tet*, Don Oberdorfer says that it was journalist Peter Arnett who reported the infamous quotation, "We had to destroy the village to save it". He attributed this quotation to an unidentified U.S. Army Major after the battle of Ben Tre. "Many reporters were present, but Arnett was the only one to hear the line and report it. Arnett was also the reporter who first broadcast that the Viet Cong were 'inside' the U.S. Embassy building, which they never were."

In Vietnam, there was a war correspondent by the name of Peter Braestrup. He was working for the *Washington Post*. "He'd been a Marine infantry platoon leader in the Korean War. He also holds the distinction of resigning from both the *Washington Post* and the *New York Times* in protest over the way they butchered his stories and generally slanted their coverage in favor of the Communists."

Peter Braestrup wrote a book entitled *The Big Story: How the American Press and Television Reported and Interpreted the Crisis of Tet 1968 in Vietnam and Washington* (1977). Remember, Braestrup was the Saigon bureau chief for the Washington Post from 1968 to 1973. Concerning the news media coverage of the Tet Offensive, Braestrup concluded that, "Rarely has contemporary crisis-journalism turned out, in retrospect, to have veered so widely from reality."

Ann Coulter in an op-ed piece entitled "Tit for Tet" wrote that, "By lying about the Tet offensive during the Vietnam War, the media managed to persuade Americans we were losing the war, which demoralized the nation and caused us to lose the war. The immediate consequence of the media's lies was a 25% drop in support for the war."

An American reporter, Keyes Beech, wrote that, "The media helped lose the war. Oh yes, they did, not because of any massive conspiracy but because of the way the war was reported. What often seems to be forgotten is that the war was lost in the U.S., not in Vietnam. American troops never lost a battle."

Wikipedia, the free encyclopedia, wrote concerning the Tet Offensive that, "The NVA suffered a heavy military defeat but scored a priceless propaganda victory."

Vietnam Veteran, Colonel of Infantry, Harry G. Summers wrote in his *Vietnam War Almanac*, "Initial media reports stated that U.S. and South Vietnamese army forces had been surprised and defeated. But it was not the United States that was defeated in the battlefield. It was the North Vietnamese army and especially the Viet Cong. Their 'general offensive and general uprising' had been a tactical disaster. Not only had their military forces been resoundingly defeated, but also their ideological illusion that the South Vietnamese people would flock to their banner during the 'general uprising' proved false. From Tet 1968 on, the NVA realized it would not be able to attain its political objective with guerilla forces and increasingly the war became an affair for the regular forces of the NVA." The Viet Cong were essentially wiped out during the Tet Offensive of 1968. Its cadres were decimated. In 1975, after all U.S. troops had pulled out of Vietnam, the Viet Cong guerillas could not take over South Vietnam; it took North Vietnamese Army tanks to take over South Vietnam.

What was the aftermath and outcome of the U.S. withdrawal from Vietnam? The Communist North Vietnamese army took over South Vietnam. One million South Vietnamese people tried to flee the country by boat. They were known as the boat people. Hundreds of thousands fled to Thailand on foot. America took in 750,000 Vietnamese boat people. 50,000 Vietnamese boat people died at sea.

The Communists rounded up and executed thousands of doctors, engineers, and professionals. The Domino Theory predicted by America's political right became a reality. The Communists took over not just South Vietnam, but also Laos and Cambodia. The Communists started butchering their own people in mass executions. The Khmer Rouge in Cambodia killed millions of Cambodians. Vietnam went to war with Cambodia and China. As Victor Davis Hanson wrote, "In the first two years after the fall of Saigon (1975-1977), there were almost twice as many total civilian fatalities in southeast Asia – from the Cambodian holocaust, outright executions, horrendous conditions in concentration camps, and failed escapes by refugees – as all those incurred during ten years of major American involvement (1965-1974)."

More human beings were killed in South East Asia after the U.S. troops went home, then during the entire course of the U.S. involvement in the Vietnam War. Liberals and leftists in America did not speak out against the Communist atrocities in South East Asia. They didn't care if Asians killed Asians in great numbers in order to advance socialist causes. They only protested when Americans killed Asian Communists in order to protect the freedom of other Asian peoples. Such is the rationale of the American political left.

Because of the biased media coverage of the Vietnam War, Margaret Thatcher refused to allow media correspondents to cover the Falkland Islands War alongside the frontline combat units. Ronald Reagan refused to allow media correspondents to cover the invasion of Grenada alongside the frontline combat units. George H.W. Bush restricted the access of the media in the first Gulf War.

The Tet Offensive took place when there were only three major television stations in America. They were all three left of center politically. There was no pro-American Fox News Network as there is today. That is why it is so crucial that pro-American alternative media, like Fox News and Talk Radio, should counter-balance the lies of the Left, so that an American victory, like the Tet Offensive, can never again be turned into an American defeat.

6
Gun Control in Britain

"When the Cambrian measures were forming, they promised perpetual peace. They swore, if we gave them our weapons, that the wars of the tribes would cease. But when we disarmed they sold us and delivered us bound to our foe, and the Gods of the Copybook Heading said: 'Stick to the devil you know'."
– Rudyard Kipling

In 1988 the British government banned the private possession of shotguns and rifles. In 1997 British Parliament banned the private possession of all handguns in Great Britain. The British government confiscated 162,000 registered handguns from licensed owners. Any British citizen found to have a firearm, even a "BB gun" or air rifle, after the buyback period, would be prosecuted to the fullest extent of the law. The political left said that these new strict gun control laws would reduce the crime rate. The political left promised peace in the streets of England if only the law-abiding citizens would turn in their weapons to the government.

Right after these gun control laws were implemented the crime rate skyrocketed. *The International Crime Victims Survey* put forth by the Dutch Ministry of Justice, found that England now had the highest burglary rate, robbery rate, assault rate, and sexual assault rate among the seventeen leading industrialized nations of the world. London gun murders tripled in 2001. On January 3, 2002, the *Daily Telegraph* reported,

"Police fear a new crime explosion as school-age muggers graduate to guns...the number of people robbed of personal property at gun point rose by 53 percent...Ballistics experts warn that firearms are now cheap and easily available." On December 19, 2001 the *London Evening Standard* wrote that, "Gun crime in London is rocketing, with increases of almost 90% in some firearms offenses, Scotland Yard reported today. New figures show London murders with guns increased by 87% in the first eight months of the year compared with the same period last year."

According to the *UN Interregional Crime and Justice Research Institute Report*, issued in July 2002, England and Wales had the highest violent crime rate in the Western World. The *Independent* wrote that, "Britain is now the crime capital of the West."

During the same time period that robberies rose by 81% in England and Wales, they fell by 28% in the United States. During the same time period that assaults increased by 53% in England and Wales, they decreased by 27% in the United States. "Burglaries doubled in England but fell by half in the United States."

Why is there such a startling difference between the burglary rates in Britain compared to the United States? It is because in the United States burglars know that they stand a good chance of being shot by the homeowner. Therefore, they rarely attempt to burglarize houses when they know that the owner is home. In Britain, daytime burglaries and burglarizing when the owner is home are commonplace because the armed criminals have no reason to fear the disarmed law abiding homeowner.

Many states in the USA have adopted right to carry concealed gun laws, which allow the average law abiding citizen to carry a concealed firearm. Professor John R. Lott of the University of Chicago proved through his research that law abiding citizens carrying concealed weapons deters violent crime. "Professor Lott found that when concealed-carry laws went into effect in a given county, murders fell by 8%, rapes by 5%, and aggravated assaults by 7%."

The burglarizing and terrorizing of disarmed law abiding British subjects has become so commonplace that even the British aristocrat and intellectual genius Paul Johnson admitted in *Forbes* magazine on February 17, 2003 that his house had been burglarized three times. He wrote against the leftwing gun control laws of Great Britain and bemoaned the fact that the political left in Great Britain not only banned guns but also banned the death penalty even for serial murderers. Isn't it interesting that today a "peasant" who lives in America has more rights than an Anglo-Saxon aristocrat who lives in Britain? Paul Johnson advises young people in Britain who want real freedom to emigrate to the United States of America. Mr. Paul Johnson is a great historian and a very wise man.

I shall end this chapter on gun control laws in Great Britain with an anecdote that illustrates how far Britain has fallen. "In 1999, Tony Martin, a 55-year-old Norfolk farmer living in his farmhouse, awakened to the sound of breaking glass as two burglars, both with long criminal records, burst into his home. He had been robbed six times before, and his village, like 70 percent of rural English communities, had no police presence. He sneaked downstairs with a shotgun and shot at the intruders. Tony Martin received life in prison for killing one burglar, 10 years for wounding the second, and a year for having an unregistered shotgun. The wounded burglar, having served 18 months of a three-year sentence, is now free and has been granted 5,000 pounds sterling for legal assistance to sue Tony Martin."

The leftwing elite in the media, Hollywood and the government wants to gradually increase America's gun control laws and eventually reach a state of total registration and confiscation. They want to turn America into Britain. They want to bring British style gun bans to America. The textbooks in the public schools lie to our children about the meaning of the 2nd Amendment to the U.S. Constitution. The leftwing authors claim that our Founding Fathers intended the 2nd Amendment only to apply to the National Guard and not to private citizens. They fail to tell our children that the militia was defined in those days in the U.S. Code as "every able bodied male 17 years of age or older." The 2nd Amendment was intended to guarantee as it states, "the right of the people to keep and bear arms."

Thank God for Wayne Lapierre, Charlton Heston, and Oliver North who have defended our 2nd Amendment rights as representatives of the National Rifle Association. If it were not for the NRA's political lobbying in Washington, D.C. America's gun control laws would be just as bad as Britain's. Then there would be no place left on Earth where the people could still exercise the Anglo-Saxon common law right, to keep and bear arms.

7
Immigration and Islamic Terrorism

"The Communists in East Germany had to build a wall to keep people in. The United States has to build a wall to keep people out. It is truly a compliment to our system."
– B. Forrest Clayton

Many of the Arab Muslim terrorists who blew up the World Trade Center on 9-11-01 were illegal immigrants. Some were allowed to enter the United States as tourists. Many of them violated our immigration laws by overstaying their student visas. Their leader Mohammed Atta was allowed into the United States in spite of the fact that he had already violated U.S. immigration laws by overstaying a previous visa. Mohammed Atta was pulled over by a policeman in Florida a few months prior to 9-11-01. The policeman gave Atta a ticket for driving without a license. The policeman had no way of knowing that Atta had overstayed his visa during his previous foray into the United States.

Randall Parker of *ParaPundit.com* wrote that, "Since 9-11-01, the United States has made visas harder to get and legal immigration methods have become harder for terrorists to use. It seems reasonable to expect terrorists to respond by pursuing illegal border crossings as some have already done." The April 7, 2003 edition of the *Washington Times* reported that at least 14 al Qaeda terrorists are in Mexico coordinating with Mexican organized crime groups, including drug-trafficking organizations, "in an attempt to infiltrate into the United States in order to launch more attacks" on U.S. soil. Dr. Martin Brass wrote that "apprehensions of OTM's have increased 42 percent according to Border Patrol spokesperson Rene' Noriega." OTM stands for "Other Than Mexican". This category includes the recent surge in Arab, Muslim, Middle Eastern men crossing over the border from Mexico: a phenomenon that did not previously exist. The Border Patrol admits that because they are overwhelmed and undermanned they only apprehend one out of every five illegal aliens who cross over the Mexican border.

On September 20, 2004 *Time* magazine's cover read as follows: "Special Investigation – America's Border: Even After 9/11, It's Outrageously Easy to Sneak In." On page 51 of that same issue there was an article entitled, "Who Left the Door Open?: Despite all the talk of homeland security, sneaking into the U.S. is scandalously easy – and on the rise. Millions of illegal aliens will pour across the U.S.-Mexican border this year, many from countries hostile to America. *Time* looks at the damage, the dangers and the reasons the U.S. fails to protect itself." How many Americans have to be killed by Islamic terrorists who sneak in the U.S. across our Mexican border before we get serious about enforcing our immigration laws?

The 9/11 Commission's final report stated that, "Two systemic weaknesses came together in our border system's inability to contribute to an effective defense against the 9/11 attacks: a lack of well-developed counterterrorism measures as a part of border security and an immigration system not able to deliver on its basic commitments, much less support counterterrorism. These weaknesses have been reduced but are far from being overcome." How many Americans have to be killed by Islamic terrorists who sneak in the U.S. across our Mexican border before we get serious about enforcing our immigration laws?

On September 4, 2004, *World* magazine reported that, "terror suspects seem to be slipping in the same way other illegal immigrants do." The Department of Homeland Security's statistics show that from 10/02 - 6/03 and 10/03 - 6/04 over 8,000 illegals from known terrorist linked states entered the United States from across our southern border. How many Americans have to be killed by Islamic terrorists who sneak in the U.S. across our Mexican border before we get serious about enforcing our immigration laws?

Newsmax.com on October 21, 2004 reported that the Honduran Security Minister Oscar Alvarez said that, "Al-Qaeda operatives are recruiting Central American gang members to carry out regional attacks and to slip terrorists into the United States." How many Americans have to be killed by Islamic terrorists who sneaked into the U.S. across our Mexican border before we get serious about enforcing our immigration laws?

The Muslim holy book is the Koran (Qur'an). The Koran states in Sura 9, verse 5, "Then fight and slay the pagans [non-Muslims] wherever you find them. And seize them, beleaguer them and lie in wait for them, in every strategem (of war)." Osama Bin Laden emphasized this verse in his sermon "broadcast by the Qatari al-Jazeera TV Network on the first day of the Muslim feast of sacrifice." Arab Muslim terrorists believe that this is the most important verse in the Koran. They follow this verse's teaching religiously. They believe that the Christians, Jews, Hindus, and Secularists must all be converted to Islam or else be put to the sword. Hence Sura 9:5 is known as "The Verse of the Sword".

Al Qaeda and Hezbollah agents are setting up shop in Mexico, Central America, and South America in order to organize massive terrorist attacks on the United States of America. They raise money by engaging in organized crime including drug trafficking. Two thirds of all illegal drugs in America come in through our Mexican border. They believe that they must carry out Allah's commands as put forth in the Koran in Sura 9:5. Joseph Farah of *World Net Daily* wrote that, "Pentagon officials have confirmed human smuggling rings in Latin America are attempting to sneak al-Qaida operatives into the U.S."

We must never forget what Samuel P. Huntington wrote prior to 9-11-01, "Islam has bloody borders." Robert Spencer wrote that, in just the last few years "Muslims have slaughtered millions of Hindus in Bangladesh, Kashmir, and India. In Pakistan, they have regularly targeted Christians for violence. Thousands of Christians were killed in Cyprus during the 1974 Turkish takeover of the northern part of the island. Muslims in Iraq have massacred Assyrian Christians sporadically during the nineteenth and twentieth centuries. Conflicts rage today between

Muslim and non-Muslims in Indonesia, the Philippines, and elsewhere."

Huntington wrote that, "In the early 1990's, Muslims were engaged in more intergroup violence than were non-Muslims, and two-thirds to three-quarters of intercivilizational wars were between Muslims and non-Muslims. Islam's borders are bloody, and so are its innards." Are these the people we want to have easy illegal access over our unsecured Mexican border?

Some people claim that the 9-11 terrorist hijackers could not have been truly faithful Muslims because they wore Western style clothes, were clean shaven, and they went to American strip clubs in order to have lap dances and have sex with American prostitutes. People who say this have no understanding of the Muslim concept of the sect of Takfir wal Hijra. It means "excommunication and exile".

According to Takfir ideology crime becomes a means of redemption. According to Gene Edward Veith, "Outwardly, members appear to be excommunicated from Islam, conforming to Western ways and even Western vices. But inwardly, they are devout Muslims in exile in a strange land. This split between their outward behavior and their inner piety is justified, according to Takfir theology, as a tactic of Jihad." Remember Sun Tzu wrote that, "All warfare is based on deception." Sun Tzu wrote "when strong feign weakness, when weak feign strength." The Takfir's believe when devout feign sinfulness, when sinful feign devoutness.

Sebastian Rotella of the *Los Angeles Times* wrote that, "Takfiris accept drinking and vice and encourage short hair, fashionable dress, and an outwardly Western lifestyle as a holy warrior's disguise against detection. In the Takfir creed of outward conformity and internal exile, crime is a means of waging war against the West."

Chuck Colson says that one of the most fertile recruiting grounds for Muslim Takfirs is prisons. As Veith wrote, "A Takfir imam can offer a criminal in prison a redemption that allows them to remain criminals." Their criminal energies are redirected to help the cause of Islam and the defeat of the infidel West. De Bousquet de Florian, the French Chief of Intelligence said, "Crime that was once practiced with no trace of an Islamic reference, once they have converted, rather naturally acquires an objective, a justification, a religious legitimization."

The leader of 3-11-04 terrorist attack on Spain, which altered their election, was a radical Islamic Jihadist who was also a drug dealer "who traded a load of hashish for the explosives that killed 191 people."

The one sure way a Muslim criminal can go to Paradise, according to his religion, is to die as a "martyr" while killing enemies of Allah. Our wide-open unsecured Mexican border will give these Islamic extremists ample opportunity to fulfill their mission in life.

Gene Edward Veith writes that, "Takfir may have a direct relationship to the hashishiyyin, the Muslim sect that would consume hashish as a prelude to the murder of enemy leaders, from which we get the word assassin." Do we have the political will to secure our borders in order to safeguard our people from the modern day Muslim assassins?

Is the United States a sovereign nation-state if it does not control its own borders? As of August of 2003, there were 4.5 million illegal alien Mexicans living in the United States. Almost nothing is being done to deport them. Almost nothing is being done to secure the Mexican-U.S. border. United States sovereignty is slipping away.

The former Governor of Colorado, Richard D. Lamm wrote that, "A nation must have a border, just as a house must have walls and a door. The basic element of national sovereignty is the power to control admission into a country. All countries must set limits on who can and will enter and become citizens. The United States, by this definition, today just barely qualifies as a country." The U.S. must secure its borders to regain its national sovereignty.

Massive third world illegal immigration into the United States has led to huge increases in the crime rate. Victor Davis Hanson, in his book *Mexifornia*, cited the fact that, "Almost one-quarter of California's inmates are from Mexico, and almost a third of recent drug trafficking arrests involved illegal aliens. In addition, Fidel Castro took advantage of President Jimmy Carter's do-gooder liberalism. In the Mariel Boat Lift, Fidel Castro sent the United States his entire common criminal population and his entire known homosexual population. Is this carrying the "wretched refuse" idea to an extreme? (17 years after the Statue of Liberty was dedicated, Emma Lazarus' poem was added to it. It forever altered the meaning of the statue. It states in part, "Give me...the wretched refuse of your teeming shore.")

As a result of Jimmy Carter's acceptance of the marielitos the crime rate skyrocketed in Miami, Florida and New York City. In New York City, for example, 214 Cubans were arrested in the year prior to the 1980 Mariel Boat Lift. In the year after the boatlift 2,000 Cubans were arrested in New York City. Jimmy Carter thought he was merely following the dictates of the Statue of Liberty's inscription, bringing what he perceived to be "wretched refuse" to America's shore. Maybe Jimmy Carter should have followed the U.S. Constitution written by our Founding Fathers instead of following the Statue of Liberty's inscription written by Emma Lazarus. For the Constitution states in Article IV; section 4 "The United States shall guarantee to every state in this union a republican form of government, and shall protect each of them against invasion."

What is the U.S. Government doing to protect its citizens in the southwestern United States from illegal immigration invasions from Mexico? Pat Buchanan in his book *The Death of the West* stated that he visited Douglas, Arizona, a border town southeast of Tucson. Buchanan writes, "While there, I visited Theresa Murray, an eighty-two year old widow and great-grandmother who lives in the Arizona desert where she grew up. Her ranch house is surrounded by a seven-foot chain link fence that was topped with coils of razor wire. Every door and window has bars on it and is wired to an alarm. Mrs. Murray sleeps with a .32-caliber pistol on her bed table, because she has been burglarized thirty times. Her guard dogs are dead; they bled to death when someone tossed meat containing chopped glass over her fence. Theresa Murray is living out her life inside a maximum-security prison, in her own home, in her own country, because her government lacks the moral courage to do its duty and defend the borders of the United States of America."

Buchanan goes on to write, "If America is about anything, it is freedom. But as Theresa Murray says, 'I've lost my freedom. I can't ever leave the house unless I have somebody watch it. We used to ride our horses clear across the border. We had Mexicans working on our property. It used to be fun to live here. Now it's hell. It's plain old hell.'"

American soldiers defend the borders of Korea, Kuwait, Kosovo, and Iraq. Why do they not defend the borders of the United States of America?

Many first generation immigrants work very hard to earn money doing backbreaking manual labor. But many of the 2nd and 3rd generation, those who were born on U.S. soil, can enroll in welfare programs and become an economic drain on society. Peter Brimelow proved that massive third world immigration causes the welfare rolls to dramatically increase in size. Brimelow wrote in 1995 that, "In California, fully a third of all public assistance goes to immigrant-headed households." Today the problem is even worse. Victor Davis Hanson wrote in 2003 that there is an "overrepresentation of Mexican-Americans in our jails, prisons, and welfare programs."

Healthcare costs including bills for hospital stays are skyrocketing, partially due to the fact that illegal immigrants go straight to the emergency room for all their health care needs. They are treated. They never pay their bill. They don't have the money to pay it. They are uninsured. Tax paying legal American citizens must pick up the tab – through higher health care costs. Nothing is free. Somebody has to pay the bill.

Former Governor Richard D. Lamm wrote a book entitled *The Immigration Time Bomb*. In that book he lamented the splintering of our society due to massive levels of illegal immigration without sufficient time or energy spent on assimilation. Governor Lamm wrote, "Massive immigration involves serious and profound social and cultural dangers. The United States is not immune to the trends that have affected and altered all other human societies. Civilizations rise and civilizations fall- and there are certain universal pathologies that characterize the fall of history's civilizations. Ethnic, racial, and religious differences can become such a pathology; they can grow, fester, and eventually splinter a society."

Lamm goes on to lament the fact that assimilation is not always taking place. "And if Americanization is breaking down, we should examine the process of immigration itself. One very good reason that immigrant groups may not be accommodating themselves to this country may be that the pace of immigration into certain cities and states is too rapid, that the continuing immigration stream is preserving the separatism of migrant groups. Both acculturation and immigration, after all, are demographic processes. They can be measured by numbers. We ignore those numbers at our peril. We cannot willfully pretend that those numbers have no relevance to our country, that America is uniquely immune to profound demographic change."

Victor Davis Hanson wrote that, "A recent *Zogby Poll* revealed that 58 percent of Mexican citizens believe that the territory of the United States' southwest rightfully belongs to Mexico." Do most people of Mexican origin living in the United States feel that they are Americans first or Mexicans first? According to Patrick J. Buchanan at the Los Angeles Coliseum many of the Mexican-American fans "curse our players, shout down our national anthem and chant Osama! Osama! when the Mexican team scores."

Victor Davis Hanson attempts to console us by writing that, "If Californians complain that the children of aliens claim they are Mexicans, not Americans, and cheer visiting Mexican soccer players while booing their American athletes, they should remember that Algerians do the same thing to their hosts in France, as Pakistanis often do in Great Britain, and as Turks do in Germany." Rudyard Kipling called this, "The blame of those ye better, the hate of those ye guard." Many of these people are ingrates. Their jealousy leads them to hate their benefactors. Blood and religion are often times thicker than soil and water.

A more profound problem is that of language. Over the past twenty years most legal and illegal immigrants into the United States

speak only one language. They speak the
Spanish language. Many of these immigrants
refuse to learn English, and bilingualism is
creeping in. Governor Lamm movingly wrote that,
"I am concerned about the dangers of countries in
which two language groups clash. I think about
the problems caused by Quebec's separatist
movement, founded upon the French language. I
think about the tensions even within peaceful
multilingual countries: the cantonization of
Switzerland and the division of Belgium.
Language is clearly the cause of some of the
world's most severe tensions and disputes." The
Shakespearian English of the King James Bible
once unified our culture. A Tower of Babel now
divides us.

The political and academic left supports the
concept of the Tower of Babel under the
euphemistic name of "multiculturalism". Victor
Davis Hanson rather astutely observed that,
"Since roughly 1970, the evolving concept of
multiculturalism- which holds that Western
Civilization merits no special consideration
inasmuch as all cultures are of equal merit – has
proved to be the force – multiplier of illegal
immigration from Mexico."

In order to promote multiculturalism, the
leftists write history textbooks that over-
emphasize the flaws of the United States in
particular and Western Civilization in general and
suppress information concerning the flaws of
third-world cultures. Victor Davis Hanson said
that, "The result of the whitewashed new history
is that Aztec cannibalism and human sacrifice
(especially at the dedication of the great pyramid

of Huitzilopochtli in 1487) on a scale approaching the daily murder rate at Auschwitz are seldom discussed as a part of the Mexican past. While Cortes is loudly condemned, we do not hear that the Tlaxcaltecs and other tribes considered the Europeans saviors rather than enslavers."

Leftwing professors have turned our college campuses into hotbeds of multicultural indoctrination. Victor Davis Hanson says that the liberal elites "wrongly think that we can instill confidence by praising the less successful cultures that aliens are escaping, rather than explaining the dynamism and morality of the civilization that our newcomers have pledged to join." Hanson says that the public schools are "hostile to the Western paradigm."

Hanson does a good job of diagnosing the psychopathology of the liberal elites. They suffer from a general guilt complex and a form of masochism. Hanson says that in California the universities encourage "white" students to take courses that promote bilingualism, affirmative action, and reparation payments. Hanson uses the term "masochism" to describe the psychology behind the white liberal professors who teach these courses. Hanson says that the leftist professors "reject any unifying core" for our nation state. The result of radical multiculturalism will be what William Butler Yeats describes so eloquently in one of his poems, "The center can not hold, mere anarchy is loosed upon the earth." How can the center hold without a unifying core?

Hanson also understands the power of music over the lives of young people. He wrote,

"Scholars must stop teaching nonsense like the idea that...gangsta rap is essentially no less musical than Beethoven." He realizes that this pernicious form of multiculturalism is destroying our culture, and might eventually destroy our nation-state.

Hanson bemoans the fact that most students graduate from high school in California knowing who Caesar Chavez and Susan B. Anthony are, but they have never heard of MacArthur or Patton. Military history is suppressed while social history is emphasized. That is the preference of the leftwing professors who write the history textbooks. Military history questions were banned from the National Advanced Placement Test in U.S. History. These are tests in which our best and brightest high school students compete for college credits.

What are the political ramifications of our open-borders immigration policy? Let us look at the statistics. In the 1992 presidential election Bill Clinton won 39% of the white vote, 82% of the black vote, and 62% of the Hispanic vote. Based on that performance he became President of the United States. In the 1996 Presidential election Bill Clinton won over 70% of the Hispanic vote. In the Presidential election of the year 2000, Al Gore won 62% of the Hispanic vote. This massive increase in the Hispanic population of the United States due to our open borders immigration policy is making it much more difficult for a Republican to win the White House. Remember George W. Bush speaks Spanish fluently, his brother Jeb has an Hispanic wife and son, and he is for open immigration from Mexico. In spite of all these facts, Bush the Republican won only 35% of the Hispanic vote in 2000 and approximately 43% of the Hispanic vote in 2004.

There are patriotic Americans of all races. The problem is not racial; it is cultural. Multiculturalism is defeating the process of assimilation. Without proper assimilation new immigrants cannot succeed. Without proper assimilation the United States as a nation-state cannot succeed.

What can be done to solve this immigration problem? What can be done to stem the tide and prevent terrorist attacks? According to John Leo, in *U.S. News and World Report*, "A 2002 Zogby poll showed that 68% of Americans are so anxious about illegal immigration that they want to deploy troops along the border." The United States should build a Berlin Wall type structure on its Mexican border and have it manned by at least one U.S. Army Division. This would drastically reduce the number of illegal aliens who enter our country and dramatically improve our national security posture.

Some may say, "You can't do that," "Berlin Walls are what the Communists build." "We are not Communists, so we shouldn't build a Communist type wall." Well, it is true that the Communists built the Berlin Wall, but the wall that this author is proposing is just the opposite. It is the Berlin Wall in reverse. The Communists had to build one to keep people in. The United States has to build one to keep people out. It is truly a compliment to our system.

Mort Zuckerman, the editor of *U.S. News and World Report*, wrote on August 2, 2004 that,

"Indeed, building a fence is one of the most civilized ways in which nations can defend themselves, in Shakespeare's words, 'against the envy of less happy lands,' when they share a border with armed attackers who lack an effective government to constrain them." In the year 2004, the Israelis built a wall, which has greatly improved their national security posture by saving many lives. Zuckerman wrote that, "Terrorist penetration into Israel from the northern West Bank, where the initial portion of the fence was completed, has dropped from 600 a year to zero – as Israel was able to foil every suicide bombing originating from the northern West Bank and specifically from the cities of Mablus and Jenin, areas that had previously been infamous for exporting suicide bombers."

We need a wall on our southern flank. All other proposals short of that are only half measures that won't solve the problem. Robert Frost used to help his neighbor mend the stone wall that divided their property. He wrote a poem about it called "Mending Wall". He started his poem by saying, "Something there is that doesn't love a wall." But we should never forget how Robert Frost ended this poem. He ended it with the wise advice, "Good fences make good neighbors."

Introduction to Social History

Even though the issues in this section are not suppressed in the same way as the other issues discussed in this book, these cultural issues are part of the "politically correct paradigm."

8
The Decline of Dress, Speech, and Manners

"The privileged class took on the speech, dress, manners and immorality of the lower classes."
– Edward Gibbon- The Decline and Fall of the Roman Empire

Language and dress are the outward manifestations of a culture. Eloquent language and dignified dress are hallmarks of a great civilization. Vulgar language and undignified dress are hallmarks of a gutter people, barbaric, and uncivilized. A culture that goes from formality in dress, speech, and manners to extreme casualness in dress, speech and manners is a culture in decline. The great chronicler of *The Decline of the Roman Empire*, Edward Gibbon, had it right when he wrote, "It is the mark of a civilization in decline when the upper classes start to imitate the dress, speech, and manners of the lower classes."

Casual attitudes towards dress, speech, and manners usually accompany casual attitudes towards morality, responsibility, and discipline. In Ancient Rome the decline in dress, speech, and manners accompanied a rise in "bread and circuses". The "bread" represented a growing socialist welfare state and the "circuses" represented perverted entertainments in the circus maximus and the coliseum, like feeding Christians to the lions while the masses cheered for more satanic violence to satiate their lust for cheap entertainment.

In the late 1960's and early 1970's, the leftwing hippie movement started its cultural revolution in the United States and was later successful in taking over much of the entertainment media. In the United States casual attitudes towards dress, speech, and manners accompanied casual attitudes towards "drugs, sex, and rock n roll." If "Liberty, Equality, and Fraternity" was the battle cry of the French Revolution, "Drugs, Sex, and Rock n Roll" was the battle cry of the hippie movement. The long hair of the hippie movement is no longer with us, but the drugs, sex and rock n roll music of the hippie movement have taken over our popular culture and remain with us to this very day.

The hippie movement emphasized the idea that formality in dress, speech, and manners was bad and that casualness in dress, speech, and manners was good. Our society today has clung steadfastly to this new radical belief system. This rebellious attitude instilled in our culture by the hippie movement has led to much higher levels of libertine style liberalism. For example, one of the leading leftwing propagandists in America today, Michael Moore, goes out of his way to appear unshaven, unpressed, and unkempt.

Dignified dress and eloquent use of language show respect for oneself and respect for others. Casualness shows a lack of respect for oneself and others. It has been said, "You can't show respect for anyone else when you don't respect yourself."

I read an interesting anecdote recently concerning an eleven-year-old girl who does indeed have respect for herself, her family, and her God. This young American girl was shopping for a pair of jeans at a Nordstrom's Department store. Her name is Ella Gunderson and this is what she wrote, "Dear Nordstrom, I'm an 11-year-old girl who has tried shopping at your store for clothes, in particular jeans, but all of them ride way under my hips, and the next size up is too big and falls down. They're also way too tight, and as I get older, show everything every time I move. I see all of these girls who walk around with pants that show their bellybutton and underwear. Even at my age, I know that that is not modest. With a pair of clothes from your store, I'd walk around showing half of my body and not fully dressed. Your clerk suggested there is only one look. If that is true, then girls are supposed to walk around half-naked. I think maybe you should change that." The political left that controls our popular culture wants our little girls to dress like prostitutes. They want our girls to have the choice to get an abortion but not the choice to dress in a dignified and modest manner. Britney Spears is in. June Cleaver is out.

The *News Hour* with Jim Lehrer on PBS frequently features a political commentator by the name of David Brooks. Mr. Brooks on page 56 of his book *On Paradise Drive* states that, "It's a brightly colored scene – *Abercrombie and Fitch* spaghetti-strap tops on the girls and ankle-length canvas shorts and lace-less Nikes on the boys. Patio man notes somewhat uncomfortably that in America today the average square yardage of boys wear grows and grows, while the square inches in the girls' outfits shrinks and shrinks. The boys carry so much fabric they look like skateboarding

Bedouins, and the girls look like preppy prostitutes." David Brooks was a senior editor at the *Weekly Standard.* He now writes op-ed pieces for the *New York Times.* Brooks is the modern day chronicler of America's popular culture. He admits in his book that the average American girl is supposed to dress like a prostitute, according to the fashionistas at *Abercrombie and Fitch.*

In the year 2004, at Super Bowl XXXVIII, *CBS*, *MTV*, and *Viacom* ambushed 90 million people by putting forth a surprise attack halftime show that included the desecration of the American flag, crotch grabbing, foul language, full frontal nudity and a simulated sexual assault. They gave no prior warning. Britney Spears and Janet Jackson are held up as role models by the popular culture for our daughters and granddaughters to imitate. They are supposed to show their bellybutton to all the boys as Britney did and show their breasts to all the boys as Janet did.

Today, according to *World Net Daily* a company in Los Angeles "Brands on Sale" is selling "Pimp and Ho" costumes for little kids to wear for Halloween. Costume creator Johnathon Weeks said "Kids don't even know that the word pimp means – regarding soliciting women for sex. They think being pimp means have big, fancy cars and homes." Rappers like to use the term "ho" to describe women. "Ho" in their slang is short for the word whore. *MTV,* owned by *Viacom,* has a show entitled "Pimp my Ride". Apparently *Viacom* wants our children to use vulgar slang language and dress like "pimps" and "hos".

David Kupelian of *World Net Daily* wrote, "Just as the military and private schools and Boy Scouts have uniforms, so does the youth culture: baggy pants, backward hats, chokers and other jewelry, body piercing, tattoos and the like. But if uniforms symbolize values and allegiance, a loyalty to a higher (or lower) order, then in this case it's an allegiance to an increasingly defiant musical, social, sexual and cultural world, a mysterious (to parents) realm that seems magically to be drawing millions of children into it." The uniform of rebellion during the 1960's, 70's, and 80's was modeled by the Rock 'n Roll stars of that era. The uniform of rebellion in the 1990's and the first part of the twenty first century is modeled by Rap/Hip-Hop stars.

Patricia Hersch in her work, *A Tribe Apart: A Journey into the Heart of American Adolescence* wrote that, "It's hip-hop in suburbia, the culture of rap. Everywhere students wear baseball caps turned backwards or pulled down over their eyes, oversize t-shirts, ridiculously baggy jeans or shorts with dropped crotches that hang to mid-shin, and waists that sag to reveal the tops of brightly colored boxers. Expensive name-brand high-tops complete the outfit. Variations on them are hooded sweatshirts, with the hood worn during school, and 'do rags', bandannas tied on the head, a style copied from street gangs. Just as ubiquitous are the free-flying swear words, sound bursts landing kamikaze-style, just out of reach of hall guards and teacher monitors."

Patricia Hersch also wrote that, "In the latest exasperating challenge to adult society, black rage is in as a cultural style for white middle-class kids...Today's adolescents have co-opted inner-city black street-style as the authentic way to be. To act black, as the kids define it, is to be strong, confrontational, a little scary... 'We are living in the gangsta generation', one white high school senior wearing his Malcolm X baseball cap turned backwards explains."

Hersch goes on to tell us that, "Hip-hop's in-your-face attitude looks strong and free to kids who feel constrained by expectations of the mundane middle-class world they have grown up in. Rappers have become the most popular attractions on MTV. In an interview on his album *Home Invasion*, rapper Ice T refers to the 'cultural invasion' that is occurring while unknowing adults sit around...and their kids sit quietly in their bedrooms, his words pouring into their brains through their headphones: 'Once I get 'em under my f—kin' spell/They may start giving you f—kin' hell' he raps. 'Start changin' the way they walk, they talk, they act/now whose fault is that?' The rap world of 'hos and pimps, bitches, mutha f—ckers, homey and police' is an attractive diversion from the 'ordinary' sphere of dental braces, college boards, and dating. The ghetto-experienced second-hand in movies and music and on the evening news, viewed from the comfort of nice suburban family rooms – holds enormous drama and appeal for young people." Too many young people today want to dress, speak, and behave like hip-hop gangsta rappers and too few young people today want to dress, speak, and behave like Condoleezza Rice, or Billy Graham. For Viacom does not promote good Black role models; it merely promotes bad Black role models. Most of these young suburbanites have never heard of Condoleezza Rice, but they can quote verbatim from memory the rap lyrics from Eminem.

William Shakespeare wrote that a young man should, "Dress rich, but not gaudy, for the apparel oft proclaims the man." Today's hip-hop fashions are gaudy and they proclaim that their wearer is a fool. The leftwing professors at Georgetown University in Washington, D.C. eliminated Shakespeare from their list of required courses for English Literature majors. They thought that Shakespeare was a dead white male who was far too conservative for their required curriculum. In choosing curriculum on many college campuses today leftwing ideology is paramount and talent is irrelevant.

Poor dress often times leads to poor manners. I remember I was shocked one Sunday morning at church recently when the preacher told the congregation not to leave their used paper coffee cups on the floor or in their chairs, because they were having to waste too much time cleaning up the litter after the church service. When people used to wear suits and ties to our church and it was against the rules to bring food or beverages into the sanctuary we never had that problem.

I'll never forget a recent Sunday morning at church when the guest preacher wasted the first four minutes of his sermon apologizing profusely to the congregation for wearing a suit and tie. The regular ministers were dressed casually and most of the audience was dressed casually. The guest preacher felt embarrassed and overdressed for the occasion. He told the people that he didn't get the word concerning the proper dress code and he begged the audience not to think that he was stuffy because he was wearing a suit and tie. He said that when he counsels married couples he does not wear a suit and tie, but usually dresses casually so you could trust him and relate to him.

It used to be at my church that only old men in suits and ties could serve communion. It used to be that the church service was held in a carpeted formal sanctuary; now it is held in a gymnasium. It used to be they played beautiful old hymns; today they almost exclusively play rock music.

Dennis Prager wrote that his radio show's producer went to a high school graduation ceremony and that "he was the only man in the audience wearing a jacket and tie." Prager wrote, "Only in an age that rejects wisdom could most people believe clothing is unimportant."

In the movie *Pretty Woman* Richard Gere told the prostitute character played by Julia Roberts to take his credit card and buy some "conservative" clothes. She responded, "You mean boring?" Gere responded, "No, I mean classy." Young people should be taught to dress conservatively. Older people should lead by example.

An African American conservative intellectual by the name of Thomas Sowell wrote, "One of the signs of our times is a lawsuit by the American Civil Liberties Union against the Albuquerque public schools for having a dress code which prohibits students from wearing sagging trousers that show their underwear. The ACLU attorney in this case does not wear sagging trousers. The client is a black teenager, but his white lawyer is impeccably dressed in suit and tie...This recalcitrant kid in sagging pants is the mascot of the white lawyer in the business suit. For years to come, this kid may pay the price of looking like a bum, while the well-dressed lawyer will make a statement-ultimately at the kid's expense."

Thomas Sowell went on to write that, "The tragedy is when mega-bucks morons become role models for millions of minority youngsters, only a handful of whom will ever be able to turn gutter talk and garish behavior into dollars and cents. Far more youngsters are likely to find this garbage leading only to a long slide downhill that can end on the welfare rolls or in prison.

Meanwhile, the people in their suits and ties will have enjoyed these mascots and may also be able to enjoy their affluence with a clearer conscience for having stood up for the poor and the downtrodden." Mr. Sowell understands that the white liberal intellectual is a guilt-ridden creature that attempts to salve his conscience through implementing leftwing programs intended to help blacks but that have the unintended consequences of making their problems worse. To use modern 12-step program language, they are enablers. Leftwing liberal intellectuals engage in what President George W. Bush calls "the soft bigotry of low expectations". They do not expect a young black male to be able or willing to dress in a dignified manner, so they defend his "right" to dress as a bum.

I watched the summer Olympic games of 2004 on television every night with my wife and children. It was my daughter's first chance to see the Olympic games. The backdrop was Athens, Greece. There was history, pageantry, and sports to learn about and experience through the wide eyes of a curious three-year-old girl. Unfortunately, my daughter was presented with bad examples on our TV screen, just as she had been during the Super bowl halftime show of 2004. This time it was less blatant but more insidious.

We were watching the 400-meter running race, which was won by a white American who wore a large gaudy diamond earring in each of his ears. He also wore what the rappers call "bling-bling" but what is referred to in standard American English as necklaces. My daughter looked up at me and said, "Daddy, are boys supposed to wear earrings?"

We also watched two American white women win the gold medal in the beach volleyball tournament. The one American volleyball player had a highly visible tattoo on the back of her shoulder. My daughter exclaimed, "Look at her tattoo." Children always seem to notice the details.

I always considered the Olympic games, the Super Bowl, and church to be good places to take one's family or to watch on TV. But today the perversions of the popular culture have infiltrated all of these institutions. The Marxist philosopher Gramsci was brilliantly evil when he noted that the most effective way for the Marxists to take over society was not through political elections or military coups d' etat but through infiltrating the cultural institutions that disseminate the values to the youth. Change the culture and you change the world.

Self-mutilation and defacing one's own body is going mainstream in our current popular culture. The Bible says our bodies are our temples. If we are willing to defile our churches with rap music, then it follows that we are willing to defile our bodies with multiple piercings, brandings, and tattoos.

Gene Edward Veith of *World* magazine wrote that many parents today "are apparently ok with their daughters dressing like belly dancers without the veils. And parents have no problem with their sons getting tattooed like Queequeg and pierced like Moby Dick." Herman Melville's character Queequeg was a pagan. Our leftwing popular culture is promoting paganism and attacking Christianity. As Mel Gibson said, "We are living in an age where everything is tolerated except Christianity."

There is something terribly wrong with our popular culture when our young people are encouraged to become tattooed like a pagan, pierced like a whale, and branded like a cow. Actual branding has become popular in college and professional basketball.

Young boys enjoy playing video games. On the game "NBA Live" which is played on Play Station II, one can customize his own tattoo. On the game "Grand Theft Auto," boys can get a tattoo, solicit prostitutes, and steal cars. On "Tony Hawk Pro Skater 4" suburban kids can also customize their own tattoos. The entertainment media wants to push our children into the gutter.

There is nothing wrong with an enlisted man in the U.S. Military getting a tattoo to better identify with his own unit or branch of service. This is a tradition that has always been seen as an honorable exception to the rule, just as Sampson's long hair due to the Nazarite vow was seen as an honorable exception to the Biblical directive that men should have short hair. But we must never forget the truism put forth in the film *An Officer and a Gentleman*, which states most succinctly that, "Officers don't wear tattoos."

Norman Cousins, the former editor of the *Saturday Review*, wrote a powerful and poetic essay for *Time Magazine* entitled, "The Decline of Neatness". In it he wrote, "Anyone with a passion for hanging labels on people or things should have little difficulty in recognizing that an apt tag for our time is the unkempt generation. I am not referring solely to college kids. The sloppiness virus has spread to all sectors of society. People go to all sorts of trouble and expense to look uncombed, unshaved, unpressed...Disheveled is in fashion: neatness is obsolete...The attempt to avoid any appearance of being well groomed or even neat has a quality of desperation about it and suggests a calculated and phony deprivation. We shun conventionality, but we put on a uniform to do it." We mostly choose between three main uniforms of our time, that of the pimp, the whore, or the casual sloppy bum. There is nothing wrong with dressing like a bum when that is all that you can afford, but today middle and upper class people often prefer to dress as bums. This is clearly the mark of a perverse culture.

It is not just dress that has declined since the hippie movement reared its ugly head, but it has also led to a decline in speech. Casual clothes beget casual language. Formality is obsolete. Norman Cousins wrote, "Slovenly speech comes off the same spool. Vocabulary, like blue jeans, is being drained of color and distinction. A complete sentence in everyday speech is as rare as a man's tie in the swank Polo lounge of the Beverly Hills Hotel. People communicate in chopped-up phrases, relying on grunts and chants of 'You Know' or 'I mean' to cover up a damnable incoherence. Neatness should be no less important in language than it is in dress. But spew and sprawl are taking over. The English language is one of the greatest sources of wealth in the world. In the midst of accessible riches, we are linguistic paupers."

Cousins goes on to criticize Hollywood for making films that constantly spew foul language, put forth gratuitous sex, and display violence for the sake of violence. Cousins knows that it is Nihilism and he does not approve. Michael Medved pointed out the "PG" rated films on average make more money that "R" rated films, but that Hollywood keeps making more "R" rated films in order to promote their pagan values.

John McWhorter wrote a book entitled, *Doing Our Own Thing: The Degradation of Language and Music and Why We Should, Like, Care.* John McWhorter is a Black man. John McWhorter is a professor of linguistics at the University of California at Berkeley. McWhorter wrote, "My argument is that the 1960's rejection of formality and its elevation of doing your own thing was a major turning point in the style of American speechmaking." Small talk tactics have become dominant, and grand elocutionary oratory has become practically non-existent. Conversational casualness in speeches is now prized over oratorical grandeur.

William Jennings Bryan was a great orator of the old school. He ended one of his most famous speeches with the Biblical reference, "Do not press down upon the brow of labor, this crown of thorns. Do not crucify mankind upon a cross of gold." As McWhorter says, "William Jennings Bryan dressed English in a tuxedo. Savio in 1964, tieless in his rumpled blazers, was using button-down English. Just a few years later, college students would be pushing English out onto the stage in a headband and jeans." McWhorter summed it up best when he compared the pre 1960's era to the post 1960's era in the field of oratory, "Speechmakers back then spoke. Today, they just talk."

Lack of formality in speech breeds a much more prevalent use of foul language. Actress Patricia Heaton walked out of the 2003 American Music Awards because she was fed up with the foul language, which was being spewed from the podium. A few days later at the Golden Globes, Bono proudly proclaimed the "F" word on national TV. Bad language is becoming commonplace on national television.

An attorney from Cincinnati, Ohio by the name of Charles F. Hollis III took a sabbatical trip to Moscow, Russia and accepted a job to teach advanced-level English to teenage and young adult Russian students at an English-language school. Hollis wrote, "I recall a specific instance when a fifteen year-old girl openly and unapologetically used the 'F' word in my class. When I admonished her for this, explaining that the use of such a vulgarity is never proper in any situation, she disagreed, insisting that it was. She contended that 'everyone talks that way', as evidenced by the colloquial usage of the 'F' word in rap songs." Rap music's influence is not just felt in the United States but all over the world.

In 2004, Bill Cosby berated young people in the black community who are "cursing and calling each other n----- as they're walking up and down the street." He also berated them for exposing their youngest children to the worst aspects of rap music. Cosby said, "When you put on a record and that record is yelling n----- this and n----- that and you've got your little 6-year-old, 7-year-old sitting in the back seat of the car, those children hear that."

An African-American columnist for the *New York Daily News*, Stanley Crouch wrote that, "Black popular culture continues to descend. The most recent and monstrous aspect of it comes, as usual, from the world of hip hop, where thugs and freelance prostitutes have been celebrated for a number of years...The elevation of pimps as cultural heroes. That's beyond degraded...with black teenagers, we have another problem, which is that street behavior is defined these days as being 'authentic' and 'not trying to be white'. Those who take that seriously have been committing intellectual suicide for years by aspiring downward...No other ethnic group has ever judged its authenticity by the lowdown ways of its scum. But in the poisonous wing of gangster rap, anything is possible." Bill Cosby and Stanley Crouch are upstanding black citizens berating wayward blacks. Who will stand up and berate the wayward whites?

The decline in dress, speech, and manners has accompanied a decline in morals. As William J. Bennett writes in his book *The Index of Leading Cultural Indicators: Facts and Figures on the State of American Society*, since 1960, illegitimate birth rates have increased more than 400 percent in the United States. In 1960, 23% of all American blacks born were born out of wedlock. In 1960, prior to the hippie movement, and prior to Lyndon Johnson's "War on Poverty", the Black family unit was for the most part still intact. In 1991, 67.9% of all blacks born in the United States were born out of wedlock. The traditional family unit has for most blacks been destroyed.

Racists would say that it couldn't happen to white people, only blacks. The racists are wrong. It is happening to whites. The traditional family unit is breaking down. For example, in 1960, 2% of all white births in America were out of wedlock. By 1991, 21% of all white births in America were out of wedlock. It is a matter of culture not race. An observant Judeo-Christian culture will have a low out of wedlock birthrate. A secular rock n roll, hip-hop, rap culture will have a high out of wedlock birthrate. Culture and behavior trump race. In the Scandinavian countries of Europe today, which are overwhelmingly white from a racial standpoint, the out of wedlock birthrate is over 50%. Secularism and socialism will, if victorious, destroy the traditional family unit. This is what Judge Robert Bork referred to as "slouching towards Gomorrah".

The great novelist Tom Wolfe recently did sociological research on our modern college campuses. He wrote an essay about it entitled "Hooking Up". He said that the traditional manners and etiquette of the dating game have been destroyed. Upper-middle class whites on the college campuses do not ask one another out on dates, but merely meet at drunken parties and immediately "hook up" i.e. have sex with their new acquaintance in their dorm room. This is the rule not the exception. The hippie movement and the feminist movement destroyed formality, etiquette, courtesy and modesty. The rule set has changed. The paradigm has shifted.

Is the decline in dress, speech, and manners happening by chance naturally, from the bottom up on its own accord, or is it being pushed, promoted, and sold by evil secular humanist merchants who control some large transnational corporations? The Bible states in Ephesians 6:12, "For we wrestle not against flesh and blood, but against principalities, against powers, against the rulers of the darkness of this world, against spiritual wickedness in high places." Let us examine the evidence to see if this Biblical quotation would apply in this particular case.

PBS, which is known for its moderation, some would even say a slight liberal slant, and its thoughtful intellectual analysis of the issues, put forth a powerful frontline documentary entitled

Merchants of Cool. This documentary narrated by Douglas Rushkoff told the truth and answered the question posed above.

PBS' *Merchants of Cool* started with the following sentence, "They want to be cool. They are impressionable, and they have the cash. They are corporate America's $150 billion dream." This documentary exposes *Viacom, Disney,* and *AOL/Time Warner* for their marketing and selling of filth to America's children. David Kupelian of *World Net Daily* in his essay "selling sex and corruption to your kids" wrote that *Viacom, AOL/Time Warner* and Eisner's *Disney* Corporation "Study America's children like laboratory rats, in order to sell them billions of dollars in merchandise by tempting, degrading, and corrupting them."

Mark Crispin-Miller, who is an NYU Communications Professor, says that, "When you've got a few gigantic transnational corporations, each one loaded down with debt, competing madly for as much shelf space and brain space as they can take, they're going to do whatever they think works the fastest and with the most people, which means that they will drag standards down."

Forbes magazine on February 2, 2004, had a cover story which read, "*Meet Your New Sales Force: How P&G, Coke, and Sony use teens to push products in homes and schools: A brilliant move – or marketing gone amok?*" Kupelian of *World Net Daily* and Rushkoff of *PBS* both say that *Viacom* and *AOL/Time Warner* are using hired "spies" in order to "infiltrate young people's social settings to gather intelligence on what they can induce these children to buy next."

John Leo of *U.S. News and World Report* says that many large corporations are engaged in the "selling of rebellion." Leo says, "Some of the worst cultural propaganda is jammed into those 60-second and 30-second spots [i.e. T.V. Commercials]." He lists a few: Isuzu Rodeo – "The World has boundaries. Ignore them." Foster Grant sunglasses – "No Limits." AT&T – "Imagine a world without limits." Burger King – "Sometimes you gotta break the rules." Outback Steakhouse – "No rules. Just Right." Don Q. Rum – "Break all the rules." Neiman Marcus – "No Rules Here." John Leo writes, "Wool used to be associated with decorum, but now 'All the rules have changed', a Woolite ad says under a photo of a young woman groping or being groped by two guys."

In the book *Rocking the Ages: The Yankelovich Report on Generational Marketing*, the authors state, "Boomers always have broken the rules...the drugs, sex, and rock' n roll of the 60's and 70's only foreshadowed the really radical rule-breaking to come in the consumer marketplace of the 80's and 90's."

John Leo also attacked Calvin Klein in one of his op-ed pieces in *U.S. News and World Report* because it put forth an ad campaign, which promoted "pedophilia chic, closely followed by a campaign that looked like heroin chic." Major corporations are openly promoting perversions and sin.

Are young people buying what the secular humanist merchants in corporate America are selling? The answer is yes. Charles Colson in an article entitled *Bankrupt at Age Twenty-Five: Marketing to Teens, Tweens, and Kids* he wrote about a book entitled *Branded: The Buying and Selling of Teenagers*, by Alissa Quart. Quart wrote that, "Those under twenty-five are now the fastest-growing group filing for bankruptcy. Financial-service companies now create teenage-oriented credit cards and cash cards."

Chuck Colson goes on to write that, "And marketers take advantage of this cash-rich audience. Teen magazines now appeal to 'tweens', those between the ages of 10 and 14. And the Cartoon Network airs commercials for MTV, a music channel for older teens and adults, during cartoons for 7 to 11 year olds. In *Branded*, Quart documents how marketers specifically target kids, tweens, and teens – even at their schools through 'sponsored' field trips and school events, like 'Coke Day'."

Why should dress, speech, and manners mean anything? Voltaire said, "Dress changes the manners". School uniforms have been shown to decrease the number of discipline problems and violent incidents at many schools that have adopted them.

How could a small exterior change have such a large impact on behavior? Rudy Giuliani as mayor of New York City brought down the crime rate so dramatically that people thought it was a miracle. When asked how he did it, he answered by saying that he implemented the "broken window" theory of policing. This theory says that law enforcement should not just spend time, money, and resources only on the big things like trying to solve murder and rape cases but that it should spend time enforcing the law on smaller things like broken windows, street prostitution, panhandling, graffiti, and low level drug dealing. By cracking down on the small things it made for an environment that was more orderly and disciplined, and lo and behold the rape, muggings, and murders decreased.

Do advertisements from major corporations really work? Ask yourself this question. Would a businessman spend millions of dollars on something every year if it did not produce for him profitable results? Their advertising campaigns are extremely successful in molding, persuading, and changing behavior.

People are persuaded to change their behavior based on images on television and the movies. For example, Clark Gable in the movie *It Happened One Night* took off his dress shirt and exposed his bare chest. He was not wearing an undershirt. Hanes undershirt sales immediately plummeted. James Dean in *Rebel Without a Cause* wore a white undershirt under his jacket. White t-shirt sales skyrocketed back up. More recently Sprite was struggling as a "second-string soft drink company" but its sales have recently skyrocketed upwards. Why? Because it "pulled off a brilliant marketing coup by underwriting major hip-hop music events and positioning itself as the cool soft drink for the vast MTV generation market."

Norman Cousins warns us that our children are being "desensitized to everything that should produce revulsion or resistance". Cousins understands that small things like dress and speech are connected to big things like human relationships. Cousins writes, "Untidiness in dress, speech, and emotions is readily connected to human relationships. The problem with the casual sex so fashionable in films is not that it arouses lust, but that it deadens feelings and annihilates privacy. The danger is not that sexual exploitation will create sex fiends, but that it may spawn eunuchs. People who have the habit of seeing everything and doing anything run the risk of feeling nothing." The pornography industry in America today now makes more money then the NFL, NBA, and Major League Baseball combined.

Traditional human relationships are being destroyed. *Newsweek* had a cover story entitled "Unmarried with Children" and reported that according to the most recent census "Fewer than 25 percent of American families are modeled on the Ward and June Cleaver nuclear family." According to Kathleen Parker, the syndicated columnist, the June and Ward Cleaver model is defined as a "married man and woman living with their biological offspring." Counter-cultural ideas have consequences.

Ronald Dahl a professor of psychiatry and pediatrics at the University of Pittsburgh Medical Center sympathizes with Norman Cousins' position that our young people run the risk of truly feeling nothing due to the over-stimulation by the perversities of the entertainment media. He said he noticed with his own children and others that they were "surrounded by ever-greater stimulation, [but] their young faces were looking disappointed and bored." The founding President of Northern Kentucky University and History professor Frank Steely used to say in his lectures, "Boredom is one of the most under rated factors in human history."

Dahl says the ever-increasing faster pace of the entertainment media is making our children burned out and bored. He says he sees many children who suffer from a "been there, done that air of indifference". He also says that this is resulting in the over medication of our youth with Ritalin being doled out to our boys to help their bored minds focus, and Prozac being doled out to our girls to help them cope with their "depression". Dahl says, "I question the role of kids boredom in some of these diagnoses." The hippie movement ethos that drugs are the answer to all of life's problems still lingers with us to this very day.

The Christian religion teaches us that human beings are born with a sinful nature. It is the important concept of original sin. For children do not need to be taught how to do what's wrong; they do that naturally; but they must be taught and encouraged to do what is right. The hippie movement rejected the idea of original sin. It promoted the idea of John Locke's Tabula Rasa or blank slate. It promoted the idea of Rousseau's "Noble Savage". They believed that children were born good and were corrupted by the patriarchal June and Ward Cleaver establishment. They believed as John Lennon said, a world "without religion" and its restrictions would be a Marxist utopia. The beatniks, the hippies, and bohemians, or what David Brooks calls today's "BoBos" all promote for our children the idea that they should rebel against traditional authority and become "noble savages" in the utopian environmentalist nirvana of the state of nature. Unfortunately though, Locke, Rousseau, and Lennon were wrong about human nature. Hobbes was correct about human nature when he stated, "Life in the state of nature is nasty, brutish, and short." Our children need Christ, not Lennon. For Lennon is a liar, and Christ is "the way the truth and the life."

Bad dress, speech, and manners are a symptom of what Mr. Kupelian calls "Defiant Paganism." The evil merchants at *Viacom* and Eisner's *Disney* Corporation want our children to dress, speak, and behave like pagan savages as opposed to Christian ladies and gentlemen. For they profit from peddling these perversions. They laugh all the way to the bank.

What are the political implications of the decline in dress, speech, and manners in American life today? John Leo of *U.S. News and World Report* says that there is a growing "secular-religious gap" in American politics. The overwhelming majority of secular people in America are voting for Democrats, and the overwhelming majority of religious people in America are voting for Republicans. For example, Leo writes, "In the 2000 Senate race in New York, two thirds of secularists voted for Hilary Rodham Clinton and two thirds of religious people voted for Rick Lazio. The study shows that the most religious states vote Republican, the least religious go Democratic." The 2004 presidential election bears out the truth of this statement.

We must take dress, speech, and manners seriously as outward manifestations of internal allegiances. We must take dress, speech, and manners seriously as indicators of the rise or fall of a civilization. We must treat dress, speech, and manners as seriously as Mayor Giuliani treated broken windows, panhandlers, and graffiti. Shakespeare said, "The apparel oft proclaims the man." I say the apparel oft proclaims the culture.

9
Music

"Nothing is more singular about this generation
than its addiction to music."
– Allan Bloom

On April 20, 1999, Eric Harris and Dylan
Klebold, two upper-middle class white teenagers,
went to their high school and murdered twelve of
their classmates and one of their teachers. They
then proceeded to kill themselves before they
could be captured or killed by the authorities.
This event is now known to history as The
Columbine Massacre in Littleton, Colorado. Eric
Harris and Dylan Klebold were outspoken
atheists who went so far as to ask one of their
female classmate victims if she believed in God.
She answered "yes". Then they proceeded to blow
her brains out.

What were the influences in the lives of
Harris and Klebold that helped to mould their
minds so that they would become dedicated
nihilists who would enjoy pulling off a murderous,
suicidal rampage? Why did this massacre
happen? Why do we have copycat violence of this
sort all over the country in our schools?

Klebold and Harris enjoyed playing video
games such as "Doom" whereby they could
engage in the realistic looking killing of others.
They enjoyed watching movies like *Natural Born
Killers* and *The Basketball Diaries*, which
promoted violence for the sake of violence. They
enjoyed Internet access to websites and
chatrooms, which gave them simple to use

directions for making pipe bombs. Eric Harris even took anti-depressant drugs.

But the thing that they were most addicted to was their music. They loved Marilyn Manson and KMFDM. They were addicted to the most pernicious, evil, and nihilistic rock music they could find. It was leftwing rock music that molded their minds. As Gene Edward Veith of *World* magazine wrote, "The Columbine killers were addicted to art forms – music, movies, and video games – that instead appealed to the thrill of violence and transgression, drawing out their brutality and their darkest impulses."

Where were the positive adult role models in their house, their church, their school, or their community? Their parents said they had no idea that their kids were building pipe bombs in their bedrooms. Today many lower-class children lack fathers in the home because of out of wedlock births, and many middle and upper class children lack fathers in their homes because of divorce. But even in upper middle class homes with two married parents, often times they both work long hours in order to make the lease payments on the multiple new huge "cars" and to pay the mortgage on the "McMansion". They do not have time to spend with their children. So they let the popular culture of television, movies, video games, and music raise their children. It at least keeps the kids occupied and out of their hair. They compensate for the lack of time they spend with their kids by showering money on them. With their money the kids can buy more pieces of merchandise spewed out by the popular culture. As Gene Edward Veith wrote about Harris and

Klebold, "Their social life was an adult-free zone of cliques and subcultures bitterly antagonistic to each other, a suburban version of *Lord of the Flies.*"

In the book *Lord of the Flies* we see what happens to young men without adult supervision. We see what happens to young men without father figures in their lives. We see what happens to a culture when the civilized values of the elder generation are not transmitted to the younger generation. The young men divide up into different cliques and start killing each other off. This has already happened to many of the American inner city poor neighborhoods and now it is spreading to the American suburbs.

Klebold and Harris were atheists who did not go to church. At school their English teacher complimented them by telling them that their rehearsal video was creative. This is the video whereby they rehearsed their killing spree. Gene Edward Veith wrote, "In their classes, Dylan Klebold and Eric Harris were praised for their rehearsal video." So much for getting moral instruction at school. The police in their community had received complaints from neighbors about them but refused to act on most of them. These boys had already been arrested by police before the Columbine Massacre but were always let go with a tap on the wrist.

These boys did not have a good male role model. They did not have a positive hero to look up to for direction or a God to give them purpose. Nature abhors a vacuum, so in the absence of good role models they picked bad role models. No one led them to God, so Marilyn Manson led them to Satan.

Parents are supposed to transmit their cultural values (i.e. religion, morals, customs, beliefs, traditions, God, family, country, honor, etc.) to their children. Why are they having such a hard time doing this today? Why aren't the right values being transmitted from the older generation to the younger? It is because of the "generation gap," created by and founded upon music. Specifically rock and roll and rap, which have spawned a separate "youth culture," cut off, disconnected and alienated from the older generations. (i.e. their parents and grandparents)

Prior to the invention of rock music in the 1950's there was no such thing as a generation gap. The popular music of the day was the same for people of all ages. There was no "teen" or "tween" subculture addicted to a different genre of music. As Veith wrote, "The notion of a 'Youth Culture' was a phenomenon of the '60's. Before then, music was made primarily by adults for adults." Prior to the invention of rock music in the 1950's, Europeans and Americans believed that music should emphasize harmony and melody, not rhythm and beat. They also believed that the highest forms of music were classical music like Mozart and Handel, hymns by Martin Luther, and marching music by Sousa. Rock and Roll changed all of this. It drove a wedge between the baby boomers and what Brokaw refers to as "the greatest generation" (The WWII Generation).

The hippie movement of the 1960's was founded upon the youthful rebellion of rock music. "Trust no one over thirty" was their mantra. Their music was characterized by a savage barbaric sexually repetitious rhythm and beat. Their new music was so sexually charged that the Ed Sullivan show would only film Elvis Presley from the chest up, for he moved his hips like a sex addicted Kennedy compound denizen. They called him "Elvis the Pelvis".

I'll never forget the ride in a van to one of my high school cross-country running races. Looking back on it, I realized that it was an anecdote, which illustrated a profound point. I was in high school. It was the 1980's. I was one of the top seven runners on the cross-country team. Our coach was driving us seven boys to a cross-country invitational at Malone College, which was a long drive from our hometown in Cincinnati. All six of my teammates brought with them Walkman cassette tape players/radios with headphones. As soon as we got in the van all six of my teammates turned on their walkmans and donned their headphones. They were all listening to their punk rock and alternative rock and roll music. They did this for the entire trip up and back.

The coach held a conversation with me for the entire trip up and back. I was the only one he could possibly talk to, for I was the only one not addicted to music. I was the only one not wearing headphones. I was the only who did not bring a Walkman onto the van. I thought nothing of it at the time

Later the coach told my mother that he really enjoyed talking to me on that road trip, but that he was disappointed with my teammates, because it was the first time in his long coaching career that he did not get the chance to talk to his boys prior to the race, not just about cross-country, but about life in general. In the past he could transmit some of his values, knowledge, expertise, and experience to his runners, but on this trip he was cut off from 6/7ths of his team. Rock music had driven a wedge between the coach and his team. The next year the coach banned all Walkmans, headphones and radios from the vans and buses. Once again he had the chance to communicate with his team.

I found an interesting article on CNN.com entitled *The Music of War*. It was about *VH1*'s documentary *Soundtrack to War*. They shot footage of U.S. soldiers in Iraq from April 2003 through July 2004. George Gittoes, the director of the documentary said, "They couldn't do it without their music." A young person today isn't supposed to be able to function without his rock and rap music. It is a perverse addiction, but one that will be noted by historians who can be in this world, but not of this world. Will the promotion of MTV values help us to win the hearts and minds of the Muslim masses? I think not. The documentary ends with "three young soldiers – all from different ethnic backgrounds," rapping about their experiences in Iraq. If rap music is our core then our core is rotten. If rap music is our center then W.B. Yeats was right – "Our center can not hold."

In the summer Olympics of 2004 held in Athens, Greece, America's greatest swimmer was Michael Phelps. I was watching the Olympics on television with my family, and I noticed that Michael Phelps had headphones on before every one of his races, right up to the last minute, and even when he was standing behind the blocks. His competitors including the "Thorpedo" from Australia did not have headphones on. The announcer Rowdy Gaines said, as the camera showed Phelps with his headphones on, "His rapper of choice tonight is Eminem." Our addiction to rock and rap music even extends to our country's greatest swimmer.

On national television when they did Phelps' biography before his first race at the Olympic games, they said that the teenager Phelps convinced his mom to buy him a Cadillac Escalade with Lattrell Sprewell rims that continue to spin after the car comes to a stop. This is known as a "pimped out Escalade" and it is one of the favorite vehicles of the rappers in 2004 America. Phelps unapologetically told the national audience that he wanted that vehicle precisely because he wanted to be like the rappers on television. (There is an *MTV* show entitled *Pimp My Ride*, which frequently features the Cadillac Escalade with Sprewell spinner rims.) Sprewell is the NBA player best known for choking his basketball coach and putting his name on rims that would "bling-bling" a car the way heavy gold necklaces would "bling-bling" a man's chest. These are the people suburban liberals such as Phelps look to for inspiration. As they say "imitation is the sincerest form of flattery."

Michael Phelps is merely a microcosm of a much larger phenomenon. In August and September of 2004, I saw a commercial on television for parents to buy their children's "back to school" clothes at J.C. Penney. The whole commercial showed young children dressed as gangsta rappers and rapping away. It was hip-hop nation for suburban kids. They want their choice in school clothes to reflect gangsta rap culture.

Where is this stuff coming from? An African American Professor John McWhorter, a linguist at UC Berkeley who authored *Doing Our Own Thing: The Degradation of Language and Music* wrote, "White people picked this up from black people in the sixties." McWhorter says this can all be summed up in the famous song lyric, "Play that funky music, white boy." McWhorter writes, "In a way that would surprise an America before 1965, 'Play that funky music, white boy' is us."

McWhorter tell us, "White America becomes a blacker place by the year...a whole generation of white young people have grown up in an America in which rap is just music, along with a new generation of 'wiggers' who deeply embrace black speech, body language, music, and dress styles. On *American Idol*, the typical white singer sings in a black cadence and musical style – with this now processed as just general pop style."

Even the rapper Mos Def said, "In terms of what certain outlets show you, it's very one-dimensional. It's not just hip-hop music – TV and movies in general are very narrow. Sex, violence, the underbelly, with junkies, prostitutes, alcoholics, gamblers. The new trend is depravity." If a gold album selling rapper like Mos Def can see the truth why can't suburban America?

Ralph J. DiClemente, PhD, of Emory University's Rollins School of Public Health did a scientific study on "how rap music videos influence emotional and physical health." His study and its results were published in the March 2003 issue of the *American Journal of Public Health.* The study found that black girls between the ages of 14 and 18 who viewed gangsta rap videos for at least 14 hours a week "were far more likely than their peers who did not watch these rap videos to practice numerous destructive behaviors. Over the course of the one year study, they were: Three times more likely to hit a teacher, over 2.5 times more likely to get arrested, twice as likely to have multiple sexual partners and 1.5. times more likely to get a sexually transmitted disease, use drugs, or drink alcohol." The popular culture is destroying many of our children.

The Bible states in Phillipians that we should think on things that are good, pure, and righteous. Gangsta rap music leads our children to think on things that are degraded, depraved, and satanic.

Plato, thousands of years ago, in his book *The Republic*, described to a tee what happened to Eric Harris and Dylan Klebold. "For we would not have our guardians reared among images of evil as in a foul pasture, and there day by day and little by little gather many impressions from all that surrounds them, taking them all in until at last a great mass of evil gathers in their inmost souls, and they know it not." The current popular culture is a foul pasture. It was this foul pasture that raised Harris and Klebold. That is why they bore such bitter fruit. The same principle holds true for the inner city child watching gangsta rap videos. What goes in often times comes back out.

Professor Allan Bloom in his landmark book *The Closing of the American Mind* wrote that, "Today, a very large proportion of young people between the ages of ten and twenty live for music. It is their passion; nothing else excites them as it does." Bloom tells us that, "Rock music is as unquestioned and unproblematic as the air the students breathe, and very few have any acquaintance at all with classical music."

I remember from my days as a high school history teacher that the quickest way to provoke a debate in class was to insult rock and rap music, which was held sacred by many of the teenagers. This was the one and only topic that would whip up the class into a frenzy. Class participation would skyrocket as they attempted to defend the one thing they held dear.

Professor Allan Bloom tells a similar story in his chapter on music. He was teaching his students Plato's *Republic*. When he started teaching philosophy many years ago his students did not seem to care much about Plato's commentary on music. But after the hippie movement his students would become "indignant" with Plato's position on music, "because Plato seems to want to rob them of their most intimate pleasure." Bloom writes, "The very fact of their fury shows how much Plato threatens what is dear and intimate to them."

So what is so controversial (post hippie movement) about Plato's passage on musical education? Bloom states, "Plato's teachings about music is, put simply, that rhythm and melody, accompanied by dance, are the barbarous expression of the soul...music is the soul's primitive and primary speech and it is alogon, without articulate speech or reason. Even when articulate speech is added, it is utterly subordinate to and determined by the music and the passions it expresses."

Bloom goes on to write, "Plato teaches that in order to take the spiritual temperature of an individual or a society, one must 'mark the music'." The West today must have a horrible fever. For in the West today classical music is almost completely dead and rock and rap reign supreme.

Bloom brilliantly states, "But rock music has one appeal only, a barbaric appeal, to sexual desire – not love, not eros, but sexual desire undeveloped and untutored. Young people know that rock has the beat of sexual intercourse...never was there an art form directed so exclusively to children."

Professor Bloom calls rock music a "gutter phenomenon". The wise Professor writes, "It may well be that a society's greatest madness seems normal to itself."

Professor Bloom says, "Rock music provides premature ecstasy and in this respect, it is like the drugs with which it is allied." We must never forget the battle cry of the hippie movement – "drugs, sex, and rock and roll." These three allies can rarely be divided. Where there is one the other will certainly follow.

Professor Bloom ends his essay on rock music by stating that young people with headphones on – filling their ears with loud rock music "can not hear what the great tradition has to say." And if they listen to too much rock music over a long period of time, when they finally take off their headphones, "They find they are deaf." They are not just literally deaf, but they are more often than not figuratively deaf. They are deaf when it comes to listening to God's laws. They are deaf to the great traditions that built Western Civilization.

Much of rock and rap music lacks melody. Much of rock and rap music lacks harmony. Rap music is not really a form of music in the traditional strict sense of the word. Rock and rap emphasize beat and rhythm. As Professor McWhorter says, "For an American brought from 1936 to today, ...one of the hardest adjustments would be a pop music harmonically barren and rhythmically barbarous."

McWhorter went on to say that rap music takes our "rhythmic fetish to its logical extreme." McWhorter also said, "rap eliminates the singing entirely." "Whatever its power over us, music centered on repeated rhythm and a vocal tone that about one in five people could produce with the assistance of retakes and splicing is closer to a preliterate pole of musical expression than classical music."

Professor McWhorter related an anecdote, which shed more light on the truth. "One old girlfriend watched me closing my eyes and swelling a bit to the main theme of Tchaikovsky's Sixth and asked, 'What are you doing?' 'Enjoying the music,' I said. 'Haven't you ever seen anyone savoring a melody?' 'Yeah, old men,' she replied –

and within the only time frame she had ever known, her reaction was perfectly understandable...Before the sixties, America knew no commercially significant music in which brute repetition played such a key role." One must have a historical perspective in order to understand that prior to the hippie movement of the 1960's most American young people were not addicted to rock and roll and rap. But unfortunately, many young people lack historical perspective, and therefore, they assume that there was always a generational gap based upon musical taste.

You may say, "I have listened to rock music my whole life, and it has not had any noticeable negative effect on me." This may be true, but we have to realize that each person has a different tolerance level. Some individuals could eat French fries, ice cream, and donuts every day and never get fat. Others have to severely limit their intake of fats and sweets to avoid becoming overweight. Some teenagers are able to listen to what Harris and Klebold listened to and not kill anyone. But Eric and Dylan could not. What they put into their minds came out as a murderous spree. Rock music does not have the exact same level of effect on everyone.

You may also say, "Just because you are not attracted to rock music doesn't mean it is bad. It is just a matter of taste." The truth is, I am attracted to rock music as much as anyone else, but not everything we are attracted to is necessarily good for us. Many children would choose French fries over broccoli, cake over fresh fruit, and soda pop over milk, but we know that diabetes and obesity in children have reached epidemic proportions. Likewise, rock music may be attractive, but too much of it can shorten your attention span, dull your mind, and deafen your ears.

Rock and roll and rap are cultural junk food. It is bubble gum for the mind. It tastes good on the surface but gives us no real sustenance. Too much sugar rots out our teeth. Too much rock and roll and rap rots out our mind. The difference between Mozart and Britney Spears is akin to the difference between Filet Mignon and cotton candy. The difference between Handel and Eminem is the difference between vegetables and arsenic. The former will improve our health and the latter will destroy it.

The church should influence the culture more than the culture influences the church. Unfortunately, in many instances today, just the opposite is taking place. When it comes to music and dress the popular culture is taking over the church. As Gene Edward Veith wrote, "When American Christians try to engage the culture, they tend to embrace the pop culture [such as] bringing rock n' roll music into the church...Christians have tended to make themselves slaves of the pop culture,...imitating its worse features." Bob Collins went so far as to pose the rhetorical question, "What good is religion that merely reflects society?" The church should have a greater impact on society than the society has on the church. If not then the church becomes nothing more than another social club, which lacks any spiritual force.

The emphasis placed on rock music in the church today should not be underestimated. There is an addiction to rock music within the church that is almost unfathomable. Let me give some examples to illustrate my point. Peter Bronson wrote that when he went to church at the Vineyard in Cincinnati, the "speakers [were] loud enough for a Who concert." He went on to say that there was a "rock band, pastor in Levis, and a congregation in t-shirts, cargo shorts, and flip flops."

Jay Tolson of *U.S. News and World Report* wrote an article about the churches today entitled, "Forget Politics. It's About the Music." In it he quoted David Stowe who said, "You can't understand American religion without understanding its music."

Pat Lemen wrote in the *Cincinnati Enquirer* that her church is now like a rock concert and that the "head-banging music" is so loud that it gives her a headache.

At the church to which I belong, they recently replaced the old hymns with "contemporary" rock music. Ever since the traditional hymns were eliminated from the regular Sunday morning worship service, the old people in the church have been forced to huddle together into a segregated ghetto (i.e. their Sunday school class) in order to sing the hymns. Apparently many of the baby boomers and their offspring can only stomach "contemporary praise songs" i.e. rock music, and therefore the hymns had to go.

Michael S. Hamilton wrote in *Christianity Today* – "The Triumph of the Praise Songs: How

Guitars Beat Out the Organ in the Worship Wars"
that, "Only a generation that loved Woodstock
could love Willow Creek." The generation he was
referring to was the baby boom generation. The
church Willow Creek in Illinois is one of the
largest churches in America, and it plays loud
rock music at its worship services.

Michael S. Hamilton wrote, "It is no
accident that Chuck Smith's Cavalry Chapel, one
of the first congregations to welcome the
counterculture, was one of the first to welcome its
music. And it is no accident that in 1973 Calvary
Chapel started *Marantha*! Music to spread the
new music to other churches. As baby boomers
moved into the churches, this music came along
too. It soon acquired a new name – 'praise and
worship' – but it began as baptized rock n' roll."

The most popular "praise song" in American
churches today is entitled "Lord, I Lift Your Name
On High." This epitomizes the contemporary light
rock n' roll "praise" songs. As Michael S.
Hamilton wrote, one cannot sing praise songs
without noticing how first person pronouns tend
to eclipse every other subject." Daniel Block, a
professor at Southern Baptist Theological
Seminary said that many contemporary praise
songs are really about praising one's self, not
praising God. For instance, the song "I Love You
God", "It's really worshiping myself. I'm praising
myself for my love for God. The other side of it is
that it's so different from the songs we used to
sing...we're impressed with our love for God,
when really we should be impressed with God's
love for us."

Hamilton wrote in *Christianity Today* that, "The starting place for the revolutionaries was secular rock n' roll, so they eagerly used guitars and drums, simple accessible lyrics, and the conventions of popular music – simple harmonies, steady rhythm, frequent repetition."

I remember being interviewed on a Christian radio talk show concerning Michael Eisner's attempt to destroy the heroic reputation of Davy Crockett through a major motion picture. The Christian conservative interviewer agreed with everything I said for almost a full hour of radio airtime, right up until the very end of the interview. His last question to me was a good one to end on. It was "Why does any of this stuff about Davy Crockett's death matter?" I responded by saying that it mattered because our children need good positive patriotic role models and heroes to look up to and emulate, ones like Davy Crockett who believe in the values of God, family, and country so that they don't look up to bad role models who promote only the values of drugs, sex, and rock n' roll." For the first time in the interview, my statements offended the Christian conservative talk show host. He said, "I agree with you on the part about drugs and sex, but rock n' roll is good as long as it has Christian lyrics." Time was up and that ended the interview.

Joel Belz the publisher of *World* magazine wrote an essay in May of 2004, which illustrates the extent of the addiction to rock music even within the Christian community. According to Belz, the addiction to rock music is so strong that it leads Christians to violate the eighth commandment "Thou Shall Not Steal" on a regular basis. "New findings from the Gospel Music Association last week [show] that evangelical Christian young people are almost as likely as their non-Christian counterparts to download their favorite music from the internet without paying for it. Maybe the basic problem isn't so much that Christian kids are so inclined to steal music. Maybe they're learning the wrong music in the first place."

Joel Belz got more negative mail for his oblique attack on rock music than he did for any other controversial subject he wrote on in that entire year. More people get more offended by an intellectual attack on rock music then they do at the murder of millions of innocent babies in the womb in America or the Muslim murder of millions of innocent Christian people in the Sudan. Their number one priority is to satiate their lust for the rhythm and beat of rock music. The heroin addict must first get his fix before he does or thinks about anything else.

So the music of the 1960's hippie movement has taken over the churches. What do the pastors of these churches say in their defense? How do they rationalize this as a good Christian thing to do? Rick Warren, the pastor of Saddleback Church in California wrote a book entitled *The Purpose Driven Life*. It sold over 15 million copies. On page 66 of this book Mr. Warren gives his rationale for and defense of rock, rap, and any other type of music that could be used in the churches. He writes, "There is no such thing as Christian music; there are only Christian lyrics. It is the words that make a song sacred, not the tune. There are no spiritual tunes. If I played a song for you without the words, you'd have no way of knowing if it were a Christian song." Rick Warren went on to write "One ethnic group's music can sound like noise to another. But God likes variety and enjoys it all."

Rick Warren's defense of this rock music addiction within the church is based upon a premise that I call "musical relativism." Just as in "cultural relativism" which states that all cultures are equal, and "moral relativism" which states that all moral codes are equal, I define "musical relativism" as the belief that, stripped of its lyrics, all music is equal. Rick Warren exemplified this belief when he said concerning music, "God enjoys it all." For, "It is the words that make a song sacred." According to musical relativists like Rick Warren the lyrics trump all other aspects of the music. According to Warren, it is only the lyrics that can make a piece of music pro or anti-God.

Anybody who has studied Plato's *Republic* and Allan Bloom's *Closing of the American Mind* knows that Rick Warren's defense of rock and rap music in the church is based upon a false premise. For as Bloom wrote concerning Plato's teaching about music, "Even when articulate speech is added [i.e. lyrics], it is utterly subordinate to and determined by the music and the passions it expresses." See, Plato understood that the most powerful aspect of music is not the lyrics, but it is the rhythm, beat, melody, and harmony. The lyrics have less impact than the rhythm and the beat. In a dance club the lyrics of the music are practically irrelevant; the only thing that matters is the rhythm and the beat of the music. The lyrics could be pro-God, anti-God, or neutral, and no one would even care or notice, as long as the techno-dance rhythm and beat continues. But change the musical genre by cutting off the rock and rap and replacing it with classical music and everyone will leave the dance floor, and a riot might ensue with demands for the sexualized beat to continue unabated.

Charles Colson and Nancy Pearcy in their landmark book *How Now Shall We Live?* do a magnificent job of setting the record straight concerning music in the church. They understand Plato's take on music and subscribe to it 100 percent. They write on page 470 of their book, "Thus rock music, by its very form, encourages a mentality that is subjective, emotional, and sensual – no matter what the lyrics may say. This is why Christians must learn to analyze not only the content of pop culture but also the art form itself, the mode of expression." For example, a person's mode of expression, how he or she says something, is sometimes more important than what he or she says. For instance a man notices that his wife is acting as if she is upset about something. She is giving him the cold shoulder and silent treatment. The man asks, "Are you upset about something?" The woman replies, "No! I'm just fine!" Her body language or mode of expression tells us that she is upset. Her words (which are akin to the lyrics of a song) tell us that she is not upset. We instinctively know that the words are subordinate to the tone and context in which they are stated.

We know that her words are subordinate to her mode of expressing them.

Colson and Pearcy write that, "There are practical steps all of us can take, beginning with disciplining our personal habits to say no to the worst of popular culture. It has so infiltrated our homes, our schools, and our churches that we must start reining it in. Churches that use mostly contemporary music in their services should consider the effects of a steady diet of simple choruses and pop-style worship songs while neglecting the classic hymns of the faith."

Chuck Colson also points out that too much MTV style rock music "fosters a shorter attention span." Colson and Pearcy wrote that much of our popular culture entertainment "erodes the skills needed for sustained attention." As a teacher I saw first hand the truth contained in Colson's assessment of the situation. It was for the post MTV generation that the medical community felt the need to coin the phrase "attention-deficit disorder."

There is new scientific evidence that proves Plato was right and Rick Warren is wrong concerning the debate on music. Musical relativists in the church as well as outside it claim that all musical forms are equal and that different opinions on music are all based purely on the subjective matter of taste. They say what tastes best to the most should be used in the church because there is no qualitative difference. They say one type of music is not objectively better than another; you only prefer one over the other as a matter of your own subjective taste. They know rock music will put more people in the

pews. Candy will attract more children than
broccoli. Rock music will attract more baby
boomers and young people than classical hymns.
Scientific research proves that broccoli is better
for a child's health than candy. Scientific
research now proves that Mozart temporarily
raises one's IQ and rock music does not. MRI
and PET Scans prove that different types of music
affect the brain in different types of ways. It is
not just a matter of subjective taste. It is a
matter of objective scientific truth.

Physicist Gordon Shaw and psychologist
Frances Rauscher proved in a scientific study
that listening to Mozart's "Sonata For Two Pianos'
in D Major" temporarily improved college
students' IQ test scores by nine points. The part
of the test they improved on was the part that
required the use of spatial-temporal reasoning
skills.

In addition to temporarily raising the IQ of
college students, Mozart's music has also been
shown to have a positive effect in many other
situations. According to Forbes magazine,
"Studies by Shaw and some of his colleagues have
shown that the Mozart Sonata reduces
pathological brain-wave activity in comatose
epileptics and improves spatial-temporal
reasoning of Alzheimer's patients. A Rauscher
study showed that rats, whose brains are
presumed to have basic neural structures similar
to those of humans, scampered through mazes
faster after being raised on repeated Mozart
Sonata recordings."

Mozart's classical music improved the
spatial-temporal reasoning skills of the human

brain. They tried the same experiment with modern music and it failed. Hence, science has proven a qualitative objective difference in music. It is not just a matter of taste. All music is not equal. Or as Mr. Orwell would say, 'Some are more equal than others."

Senator Zell Miller understands this concept and he mentioned it in his book *A National Party No More*. It was when he was Governor of Georgia that Zell Miller decided to give all women in his state with newborn babies a classical music CD.

Can we attract and motivate young people in the schools and the church without offering them junk food and rock music? I know we can. As a history teacher and as a Sunday school teacher I have seen first hand students motivated by the classics of history, literature, and music. I have excited students by reciting The King James Bible, Shakespeare, Kipling, Sun Tzu and by playing Mozart and Wagner.

Many teenagers want to rebel against the establishment. So they must be made to understand that today the establishment is politically leftwing and religiously secular. The establishment today is pro-rock and rap, for it is peddled by mega corporations like *Viacom* who hire and control Dan Rather and Howard Stern. In order to rebel against the establishment, young people must become conservatives who are against rock and rap music. That is the irony of our time.

Prior to the hippie movement of the 1960's the establishment was conservative and the rebels were liberal. Today the establishment is liberal and the rebels are conservative. We can attract young people without becoming slaves to the popular culture.

We should not sit by idly while our culture turns into Aldous Huxley's *Brave New World*. As Colson and Pearcy wrote, "Huxley feared a system where people stopped caring about the truth and cared only about being entertained. Orwell described a world where people were controlled by inflicting pain; Huxley imagined a world where people were controlled by inflicting pleasure." Huxley had the people of the *Brave New World* addicted to popular music and a drug called "Soma." Too many Americans are addicted to the pleasures of drugs and rock and rap music. They are slaves to sin, which the Bible says gives pleasure for a season, but ends in death. Janis Joplin of Woodstock fame died of a drug overdose. Elvis Presley, the King of Rock n' Roll, died of a drug overdose. Jim Morrison, of the Doors, died of a drug overdose. Kurt Cobain was a druggie who blew his brains out. How many examples do we need before we open our eyes to the truth?

The British at one time controlled China's coast by inflicting pleasure through opium dens. We should not let *Viacom* control our children by inflicting pleasurable filthy entertainments upon them. It has been said that the pornography business in America today makes more money then the NFL, NBA, and Major League Baseball combined. It controls the people by inflicting pleasure. It has been said that Colombia's leading export to the United States is cocaine. The drug lords control people's lives by inflicting pleasure. Welcome to Aldous Huxley's *Brave New World.*

Joseph Conrad wrote concerning Mr. Kurtz that, "Everything belongs to him, but the thing to know was who did he belong to, who or what could claim him for their own." The question here is whom did Eric Harris and Dylan Klebold belong to? What force could claim them for their own? What were Eric Harris and Dylan Klebold addicted to? Who or what controlled Eric Harris and Dylan Klebold? Harris and Klebold were addicted to rock music and anti-depressant drugs. Unfortunately, in the end Dylan Harris and Eric Klebold were controlled by Manson and Satan instead of Mozart and Christ. Let it be an object lesson to us all.

10
Art

"Most people can no longer expect to receive consolation from art. The Refined, the rich, the professional do-nothings, the distillers of quintessence (art critics) desire only the peculiar, the sensational, the eccentric, the scandalous in today's art. And I, myself since the advent of cubism, have fed these fellows what they wanted and satisfied these critics with all the ridiculous ideas that have passed through my head. The less they understood, the more they admired me...Today, as you know, I am celebrated, I am rich. But when I am alone, I do not have the effrontery to consider myself an artist at all, not in the grand old meaning of the word...I am only a public clown, a mountebank. I have understood my time and have exploited the imbecility, the greed of my contemporaries. It is a bitter confession, this confession of mine, more painful than it may seem, but at least, and at last it does have the merit of being honest."
– Pablo Picasso

Much of the art world has sunk into an abyss – an abyss of relativism where there is no absolute truth, no right or wrong, and no objective standard for beauty or ugliness; no objective standard for good or bad. Often times today it seems that the traditional Judeo-Christian standards based upon God's natural law have been rejected and replaced with its opposite. Hence ugliness is now considered beauty and what is beautiful is considered ugly.

What is good is considered bad and what is bad is considered good. We have entered a stage of art history akin to the world of *Alice in Wonderland* after she fell down the rabbit hole. We have entered a stage in art history where the emperor has no clothes. Highly educated leftwing elite adults are blind to the truth, but little children can see the truth with great clarity.

There is an objective truth, beauty, and goodness even if the leftwing elite rejects it. God created us in his own image. God made natural law. He made it orderly and coherent. God stamped into the brain of every human being an objective scientific standard for what is beautiful and for what is ugly. We can choose to rebel against this standard, but in order to do so, we must lie to ourselves and the world around us.

Scientific experiments have proven that there is an objective standard for beauty. As Geoffrey Cowley reported in *Newsweek* magazine on June 3, 1996, "It's widely assumed that ideals of beauty vary from era to era and from culture to culture. But a harvest of new research is confounding that idea. Studies have established that people everywhere – regardless of race, class or age – share a sense of what's attractive." The article went on to say, "In a series of groundbreaking experiments, psychologist Judith Langlois of the University of Texas, Austin, has shown that even infants share a sense of what's attractive. In the late '80's, Langlois started placing three and six month-old babies in front of a screen and showing them pairs of facial photographs. Each pair included one considered attractive by adult judges and one considered unattractive. In the first study, she found that the infants gazed significantly longer at 'attractive' white female faces than at 'unattractive' ones. Since then, she has repeated the drill using white male faces, black female faces, even the faces of other babies, and the same pattern always emerges."

What was one of the scientific measurable factors that made one face more attractive than another? The researchers said that one of the major factors was symmetry. The more symmetrical a face, the more attractive it was considered to be by both adults and infants. The less symmetrical a face, the less attractive it was considered to be by both adults and infants. The *Newsweek* article states, "We love symmetry." The same holds true for paintings, architecture, and all forms of artwork. What is symmetrical appeals to our aesthetic sense of beauty and what is lopsided and asymmetrical looks unbalanced, disorderly, chaotic, and ugly. Picasso knew that his asymmetrical abstract art was "ridiculous" but he played the "clown" in order to make a lot of money "exploiting the imbecility of his contemporaries."

Charles Murray in his book *Human Accomplishment* wrote that, "Religion is indispensable in igniting great accomplishment in the arts." The greatest artists of all time, and the greatest artworks of all time came out of Europe during the Middle Ages and later in the Renaissance. The conservative Catholic Church funded almost all of this great art during the Middle Ages. During the Renaissance the Medici banking family, a group of conservative, capitalistic, business barons, funded most of the great artists and their projects, which were almost entirely Christian and Biblical in content. (There was also much classical ancient Greek content including Raphael's highly symmetrical "School of Athens"). Just look at the Cistine Chapel ceiling, or Da Vinci's *Last Supper*, or Michelangelo's *David*, or the east doors of the Baptistry of Florence on which Ghiberti the victor, and Brunelleschi the vanquished, both produced a larger than life portrayal of *The Sacrifice of Isaac*. Behold the pictorial beauty of the Biblical anecdotes sculpted into these famous bronze doors. Oh, how the art world has changed since those days that are now gone with the wind. Art has truly been subverted and perverted.

Leonardo Da Vinci's *The Last Supper* is a good example of how Renaissance artists prized symmetry. They instinctively knew that what was symmetrical was more pleasing to the human eye as well as to the eye of the Creator. Da Vinci placed Jesus The Christ in the center of the painting. On each side of Christ are two groups of three disciples. Hence, the painting is perfectly balanced with six people on each flank and one central focal point in the middle, the fulcrum upon which our history and calendar is based. Da Vinci captured in this painting the dramatic point whereby Christ said, "One of you will betray me."

The first phase of degeneracy the art world fell into has been labeled the abstract art phase. Abstract art is known for its asymmetry. (Asymmetry means without symmetry, just as atheist means without God.)

The most famous founder of abstract art was Picasso. Paul Johnson in his book *Art: A New History* said, "Picasso was always a cynical manipulator of associates and the market...Picasso was quite capable of using his visibility to oblige needy homosexuals whose professional help he exacted in return: critics, dealers, publicists." Paul Johnson was steered away from a career in the art world by his father who told him, "I can see bad times coming for art. Frauds like Picasso will rule the roost for the next half-century."

The famous art historian Ernst Gombrich wrote an article entitled, "The Tyranny of Abstract Art". Rita Lazzaroni wrote an article in Newsweek magazine entitled, "Did a Car Hit it – Or Maybe a Train?: We should be honest and stop applauding art and architecture that any child would readily say is ugly." Gene Edward Veith wrote in *World* magazine that "artist" Martin Creed won the $30,000 Turner Prize for contemporary art for his "The Lights Going On and Off". According to Veith, "It consists of an empty room. Viewers go in and after awhile, the lights come on. Then the lights go out. That's all there is to it." They call this "minimalist" abstract art. It is so extremely minimal that it is actually nothing at all. There is no skill involved whatsoever.

Abstract art has degenerated even further into pornography and obscenity. Robert Mapplethorpe, who was hailed by the leftwing elite as the greatest creator of "homo-erotic art," pawned off obscene photographs as great art. He has a photograph of a man with a bullwhip stuck up his rectum. This photograph was hung up as great art in almost every major American city. The City of Cincinnati/Hamilton County prosecuted the Cincinnati Contemporary Arts Center for pandering obscenity, when they displayed the Mapplethorpe child porn photos and homosexual sex act photos.

The pro-sodomy, pro-obscenity, and child pornography of Robert Mapplethorpe's so called art work has been surpassed in degeneracy by blasphemous "works of art." The most famous example of this is the photograph by Andres Serrano entitled "Piss Christ". "It depicts a small plastic crucifix submerged in a glass of the artist's urine." Taxpayer money from Christians went to pay for this blasphemous "work of art." For Andres Serrano received money from the Federal Government's NEA – National Endowment for the Arts.

Why is this happening today in the art world? It is because, as Charles Murray writes in his book *Human Accomplishment*, "Today's creative elites are overwhelmingly secular. Great art requires a source of inspiration that the people who produce those entertainments are not tapping. Where artists do not have coherent ideals of the good, the work tends to be vulgar."

Is there reason for hope that a resurgence of true art may take place? Yes, there is. President George W. Bush appointed Dana Gioia to the chairmanship of the National Endowment for the Arts. Dana Gioia is a conservative artist who believes that poems should rhyme and that Shakespeare is superior to Mapplethorpe and Serrano. Dana Gioia believes in objective truth and beauty. His goal is to use the NEA, not to promote obscenity and blasphemy as it was used in the past, but as a tool to promote the classics. He wants to bring Shakespeare to the masses as it was in Elizabethan times.

But more importantly than what the federal government is doing concerning art is what private citizens are doing concerning art. A private citizen by the name of Mel Gibson, with his own money, created a film entitled *The Passion of The Christ*. The secular leftwing elites in Hollywood refused to distribute his film. The secular leftwing elites at the *New York Times* viciously attacked Mel Gibson and his family in an attempt to destroy his reputation and his film. But in the end Gibson won. His film was a spectacular artistic and commercial success. Conservative Christian churches, both Protestant and Catholic, embraced the film. Christians all over the country went to see it a great numbers. It was a pro-Christ artistic achievement unparalleled in cinematic history.

In the end, it will be heroic individuals who help to pull our culture out of the ugly, asymmetrical abyss and into a world of artistic excellence marked by goodness, beauty, and truth.

11
Noah's Flood

"I have argued for years that the world's flood myths deserve to be taken seriously – a view that most Western academics reject. But here in Mahabalipuram we have proved the myths right."
– Graham Hancock

Modern leftist academics believe strongly in a worldview based upon the twin pillars of Darwinian macroevolution and Lyellian uniformitarianism. One of the major tenets of Darwinian macroevolution is that modern man evolved from a proto-ape-man gradually over a long period of time. One of the major tenets of Lyellian uniformitarianism is that all geological change on the earth takes places gradually over a long period of time. Darwinian macroevolution rules out the idea that ancient man was as intelligent as modern man, and Lyellian uniformitarianism rules out the idea of a literal worldwide catastrophic flood.

New scientific evidence has been discovered that disproves these major pre-suppositions put forth by Darwin and Lyell; yet this evidence has been for the most part suppressed by the academic and political left. For example, in 1901, a diver discovered the "Antikythera Mechanism" off the coast of the island Antikythera in the Aegean Sea. (This island is between Greece and Crete.) The diver was scouring an ancient Greek ship, which had sunk in 65 B.C. No one really knew the significance of this discovery until British Physicist Derek Price wrote an article about it in the June 1959 edition of *Scientific American*. The title of the article was "An Ancient Greek Computer."

X-rays proved that the Antikythera Mechanism contained differential gears that were not supposed to have been invented until the 13th century A.D. The Antikythera Mechanism was proven to be an analog computer that could perform amazing scientific astronomical calculations. But academia still preaches that the first computer in world history was the ENIAC, which was built in 1946 A.D. Most world history textbooks do not mention the Antikythera Mechanism.

In 1936 excavators discovered the "Baghdad Battery" in a 2,000-year-old village on the outskirts of Baghdad, Iraq. In 1940, Willard F.M. Gray, a leading engineer at General Electric proved that the Baghdad Battery produced electricity. They also found many ancient objects in the Fertile Crescent that had been electroplated. But academia still preaches that Alessandro Volta invented the first electric battery in 1799 A.D. The Baghdad Battery invented in 200 B.C. is omitted from most world history textbooks.

On November 24, 2003 *U.S. News and World Report* published an article entitled "Barbarians get Sophisticated". This article told of the discovery of a 3,500 year old sky disk and a 3,000-year-old gold "hat", both found in Germany and both containing accurate scientific information concerning astronomy. The author of the article states, "But the sky disk and the gold 'hat' are contributing to a dramatic re-thinking of the Bronze Age, which lasted from about 2500 B.C. to 1000 B.C. Scholars say these discoveries show that, far from being barbarians, Bronze Age Europeans had a sophisticated grasp of mathematics and astronomy. 'We're developing a new paradigm in European archaeology now,' says Berlin Archaeologist Klaus Goldman. 'European civilization goes further back than most of us ever believed.'" This new paradigm has been suppressed from today's public high school and collegiate world history textbooks.

According to the *PBS* television documentary *Secrets of the Dead: Search for the First Human* (September, 2004), which interviews the cutting edge scientists of our times, the Savannah hypothesis that ape-men came down out of the trees and onto the grassy Savannah planes of Africa to walk upright for the first time has been destroyed by new archeological finds. New human skeleton finds like Orrorin prove that bi-pedalism (The ability to walk upright on two legs – not four) was there at the beginning and did not evolve over time. Scientists found skeletons that pre-date Lucy by thousands of years that are already walking upright on two legs with total human physiology. The Darwinian Biology textbook picture of the "Ascent of Man" has been proven to be bogus. This new information has been suppressed from the high school biology and world history textbooks.

The truth is ancient man walked on two legs just like modern man. The truth is ancient man was just as intelligent as modern man. The academic left will do everything in its power to suppress all evidence that supports these two truths because if the evidence gets out it will destroy a major tenet of the secular humanist faith, which is Darwin's linear view of the evolution of man.

Another major tenet of the secularist faith was put forth by Sir Charles Lyell. It is known as uniformitarianism. This is a geological theory that states all major changes on the earth took place gradually over millions of years. Uniformitarianism rules out the Biblical Flood as nothing more than a false myth. The Flood is an example of catastrophic Geology, which is antithetical to uniformitarianism.

Now, today there are three different major theories concerning the Biblical Flood. The first theory, which is the majority view within the hallowed halls of academia, is that there was no flood at all. The author of the book of *Genesis* in the *Bible* made it up. The author of the *Epic of Gilgamesh* made it up. Peoples around the globe who told of a worldwide flood were merely putting forth a fictitious myth, which was lodged in their Freudian subconscious minds. The idea of the flood did not emanate from literal truth, but only from a metaphorical truth. Only Freudian psychoanalysts could solve the riddle as to why so many people around the globe would come up with the same false myth of a Noah figure surviving a worldwide flood. As Freud taught the academic left, these were signs of the subconscious dating back to early childhood – actually regressing back all the way into the womb. As Alan Dundes, Professor of Anthropology and Folklore at the University of California, Berkeley said, "The myth is a metaphor – a cosmogenic projection of salient details of human birth insofar as every infant is delivered from a flood of amniotic fluid."

It is hard to believe that an intelligent person would espouse such nonsense. But one should never underestimate the influence of Darwin, Marx, and Freud on the modern leftwing academic.

The second major theory concerning the Biblical Flood is that there really was a flood upon which it was based, but that it was a localized flood, not a worldwide flood. The ablest proponents of this theory are William Ryan and Walter Pitman. They wrote a book entitled *Noah's Flood: The New Scientific Discoveries About the Event that Changed History.* Ryan and Pitman are geophysicists who prove in their book that a catastrophic flood took place about 7,600 years ago in the Black Sea. They proved that the Black Sea prior to about 7,600 years ago was a freshwater lake. They used coring samples to prove their thesis. They obtained these with the help of *National Geographic's* Robert Ballard and his submersibles, that at one time helped to rediscover the *Titanic* and its contents on the ocean floor. Ryan and Pitman say rising sea levels around 7,600 years ago burst through the Bosporous Valley and that the salt water of the Mediterranean Sea flooded the freshwater lake with extreme force. This massive flood killed large numbers of people who lived on the shore of what was once a much smaller fresh water lake, now known as the Black Sea. Their cities, their homes, their inventions were all swept away in a catastrophic flood that took place rapidly in a short period of time.

William Ryan said of Robert Ballard's discoveries, "This is amazing. It's going to rewrite the history of ancient civilizations because it shows unequivocally that the Black Sea Flood took place and that the ancient shores of the Black Sea were occupied by humans."

Were Ryan, Pitman, and Ballard hailed as heroes by the leftwing elite academics for their amazing new discovery? No. They were viciously attacked by the leftwing academic elite for having the gall to even partially substantiate the Bible's claim of a catastrophic flood. Ian Wilson in his book *Before the Flood* wrote, "In 1996, David Harris, director of the Institute of Archaeology at the University of London said Ryan and Pitman were 'moving into fantasy land'." The leftwing academic elite circled the wagons in an attempt to defend the sacred prophet Sir Charles Lyell and his theological doctrine of uniformitarianism.

The third major theory concerning the Biblical Flood is that it actually happened and that it was indeed a worldwide flood. The ancient flood myths are extremely similar, and they all tell of a worldwide flood or flooding. Darwin, Lyell, Marx, Freud, and most modern leftwing academics believe that the ancient peoples were too stupid to know the difference between a localized flood and a worldwide flood. This, of course, is based upon the Darwinian supposition that people today are much more intelligent and evolved than people in ancient times. This is based on the Darwinian linear view of the evolution of man. If ancient people were intelligent enough to map the stars, invent computers and discover and harness electricity would they not also be intelligent enough to know the difference between a localized flood and a worldwide flood?

One of the leading proponents of the worldwide flood theory is Dr. John Baumgardner who has a Ph.D. in geophysics from UCLA and works at the National Laboratory at Los Alamos. *U.S. News and World Report* called Dr. Baumgardner "the World's pre-eminent expert in the design of computer models for geophysical convection."

Dr. Baumgardner invented a computer program by the name of Terra. *U.S. News and World Report* (June 16, 1997), published an article entitled "The Geophysics of God: A Scientist Embraces Plate Tectonics – and Noah's Flood". The article states, "Baumgardner created Terra expressly to prove that the story of Noah and the Flood of Genesis 7:18 – 'And the waters prevailed, and were increased greatly upon the Earth; and the ark went upon the face of the waters' – happened exactly as the Bible tells it. Not only did he come up with a tool used by geophysicists around the world but his 'numerical code' actually proves the bible is correct." This information has been suppressed by the leftwing secularist professors who write the public high school and collegiate science and world history textbooks. When it comes to these textbooks, Dr. Baumgardner's theory is not allowed to see the light of day. It is censored and suppressed.

Dr. Baumgardner explains how "runaway subduction" accounts for the ocean floors tectonic plates splitting apart, sending a "giant bubble of hot mantle shooting up through the underwater midocean ridges. Which displaces the oceans, which creates a huge flood." Baumgardner says that then, "After 150 days, the bubble retreated with equal speed into the Earth, and the continents began re-emerging above the water, sending the runoff back to the oceans at around 100 miles an hour. (A very fast river with a huge erosion capacity runs at only about 10 miles an hour.) This runoff would have been sufficient to create the Grand Canyon and other massive geologic features and to deposit the various sedimentary layers in about one week." Dr. Baumgardner's pro-catastrophism and anti-uniformitarianism view of geology is unofficially banned, censored, and purged from the public high school and collegiate textbooks.

Another proponent of the theory of worldwide flooding is Dr. Glen Milne, "a specialist in glacio-isostacy and glaciation-induced sea-level change at Durham University's Department of Geology." Dr. Milne believes that at the end of the last Ice Age between 17,000 and 7,000 years ago, sea levels rose dramatically and quickly because of the melting of glaciers. Dr. Milne believes that it is scientific fact based upon his computer models that "15 million square miles of habitable land were submerged underwater," which according to Graham Hancock undoubtedly flooded many civilizations that existed at that time along the coast of every continent.

Almost all academics agree that the sea level is 120 meters higher today then it was 10,000 years ago, but most academics believe the sea level rose gradually over long periods of time in accordance with Lyell's uniformitarianism. Therefore, most academics believe that there was no major worldwide flood. But the academics in the know, who have open minds and are on the cutting edge, such as "Professor Cesare Emiliani, in the Department of Geological Sciences at the University of Miami, now realize that the meltdown of the last Ice Age was cataclysmic, not slow and gradual. So writes Graham Hancock in his book *Underworld: The Mysterious Origins of Civilization.*

Professor John Shaw, of the University of Alberta, an expert on the last Ice Age, now believes that the glacial meltdown was cataclysmic and rapid, not slow and gradual. Because Professor Shaw does not toe the uniformitarianism line he is hated by his academic peers. He said, "When I go to conferences, people yell at me, people get angry and they yell and scream, and are constantly bringing in diversions because they don't want the story to be told." At a conference in Sweden a geologist told Shaw, "Don't bring your ideas here." The academic left is against freedom of speech if anybody is talking against Darwin, Lyell, Marx or Freud. Professor Shaw gave his paper at the academic conference in Sweden, but it was "not published in the conference proceedings." They suppressed his findings. They suppressed history.

Vitacheslav Koudriavtsev, "A member of the Russian Geographical Society of the Russian Academy of Sciences" said, "The most serious argument in favour of the assumption that

Atlantis was not invented by Plato is that the time when it vanished, as indicated by Plato – about 11,600 years ago (9,600 B.C.) – and the circumstances of its vanishing described by him (the sinking into the deep of the sea), coincide with the findings of modern science about the end of the last Ice Age and the substantial rise of the level of the world ocean that accompanied it." Plato did not say Atlantis sank gradually. He wrote that, "The island of Atlantis was swallowed up by the sea and vanished in a day and a night." Plato's writings on music seem to have been borne out by modern science, why not his writings on Atlantis?

The time has come to once again take the Bible seriously not just as a guide to spiritual truth, but also as a guide to historical truth. For the two realms of truth are essentially one truth that cannot be successfully separated. Many myths are based on historical fact. Schliemann found Troy because he took seriously Homer's writings in the *Iliad*. Graham Hancock found the "mythical" six temples of Mahabalipuram, off the coast of southern India submerged underneath the waves. Graham Hancock found the six temples of Mahabalipuram because he took the local legends seriously. He believed in the ancient myths. Schliemann found Troy in 1871. Hancock found the six temples of Mahabalipuram in 2002. These two men were far apart in years but close together in ideology. They both had faith in an ancient myth, and it led them to discover a literal truth.

Graham Hancock wrote the following, which is found on page 685 of his book

Underworld, which illustrates his modesty in a time of triumph, "Of course, the real discoverers of this amazing and very extensive submerged site are the local fishermen of Mahabalipuram. My role was simply to take what they had to say seriously and to take the town's powerful and distinctive flood myths seriously. Since no diving had ever been done to investigate these neglected myths and sightings, I decided that a proper expedition had to be mounted. To this end, about a year ago, I brought together my friends at the Scientific Exploration Society (SES) in Britain and the National Institute of Oceanography (NIO) in India and we embarked on the long process that has finally culminated in the discovery of a major and hitherto completely unknown submerged archaeological site...I feel fully vindicated in the view that I have long held and expressed in my book and television series that flood myths deserve to be taken seriously and can lead to the discovery of significant underwater ruins."

Do the leftwing elite academics hail Graham Hancock as a hero of science and discovery? No. He was viciously attacked by the jealous academic elites on a BBC documentary. The producers of the documentary edited out Graham Hancock's rebuttals to his opponents' arguments against him. Therefore, they were able to portray him as a fool. Mr. Hancock launched a formal complaint, which was adjudicated by an unbiased third party (The Broadcasting Standards Commission, "An organization appointed to uphold standards and fairness in U.K. broadcasting"). The adjudicator ruled in favor of Mr. Hancock and ruled against the BBC Horizon producers for suppressing crucial parts of Mr. Hancock's testimony whereby he had presented credible evidence to refute his opponents' charges. Oftentimes the leftwing academic and news media elites do not praise "amateurs" for their discoveries, but instead viciously attack them in a jealous rage. They use the lie of omission as a weapon in order to prop up their politically correct paradigm.

The irony is that Heinrick Schliemann and Graham Hancock are not professional academic archeologists or anthropologists with PhDs. But Schliemann and Hancock are the ones who are making the great discoveries. Why is this? Many of the academic PhD archeologists and anthropologists are liberal secularists who have been brainwashed by the teachings of Darwin, Lyell, Marx, and Freud. Many anthropologists would rather teach the forged document *I Rigoberto Menchu*, because it promotes Marxist ideology, than take seriously the oral traditions or written documents that preceded Darwin, Lyell, Marx, and Freud. Lyell and his lieutenants were able to successfully brainwash the academic elite that geological change on earth is slow and gradual; therefore the catastrophic flood myths must be false. Many academics do not want to advance science, they merely want to advance the paradigms in which they have total faith – Those are the paradigms set forth by Darwin, Lyell, Marx, and Freud.

Not only politics plays a role in this, but so does race. Most PhD anthropologists and archeologists are white liberals who engage in what President George W. Bush calls the "soft bigotry of low expectations". For example, they dismissed the oral traditions, the legends, the myths, and the stories told by the dark skinned fishermen of Mahabalipuram, India. The fishermen of Mahabalipuram told anyone who would listen to "follow the fish" if you want to find the underwater temples. The fish live in there. They congregate around there. At low tide we sometimes see the tops of the spires. The white liberal professional archeologists and anthropologists did not take their stories seriously. They were so arrogant as to think "how could a dark skinned fisherman in southern India educate a white liberal academic with a PhD from America? We educate them. They don't educate us!" That is their arrogant condescending attitude that keeps them from making many discoveries that lie right around the corner, just off the coast, and under the waves.

The story of a worldwide flood is part of the history of cultures all over the world. The worldwide flood myth was found in Vedic, India, the pre-Columbian Americas, and Ancient Egypt. The people that told these stories were intelligent enough to know the difference between a localized flood and a worldwide flood. The question is whether we are intelligent enough to dismiss the Freudian psychoanalytic quackery which contends that the universal flood myths are merely a psychological regression back to the flood of amniotic fluid in the womb, and to embrace the flood as literal scientific historical truth. There comes a time when a man must use Occam's razor to cut through a Gordian knot. Occam's razor tells us that the simplest explanation is most likely the correct explanation. The Freudian explanation is convoluted quackery. The simplest explanation is that the ancient peoples meant what they said when they told of a worldwide flood. They were relating their history. They were speaking the truth. Peoples all over the world corroborated that truth.

The story contained a human hero who obeyed God and survived the flood. The Jews called him Noah. The Akkadians called him Utnapishtim. The Babylonians called him Atrahasis. The Sumerians called him Ziusudra. The Kurds called him Nahmizuli. The Armenians called him Xisuthros. The Greeks called him Deucalion. The Hindus called him Manu. Shakespeare said, "A rose by any other name would smell as sweet." It doesn't matter what we call him. What matters is that he actually existed. What matters is what he did. What matters is that we acknowledge the truth and let the historical and scientific evidence speak for itself.

12
Cryptozoology

"Behold now behemoth,...He moveth his tail like a cedar,..."
– Job 40:15-24

One may ask, what is cryptozoology? According to the free encyclopedia found online at Wikipedia.org "Cryptozoology is the study of rumored or mythological animals that are presumed to exist, but for which conclusive proof does not yet exist, or are generally considered extinct, but occasionally reported." The term cryptozoology was coined by zoologist Bernard Heuvelmans.

The free encyclopedia goes on to say, "Cryptozoology has never been fully embraced by the scientific community." That is an understatement. When the subject of cryptozoology is brought up, most leftwing academics viciously attack it or make fun of it. For the most part cryptozoology is merely ignored by the leftwing academic elites. It is usually suppressed from the textbooks. Most college graduates have never heard of cryptozoology. Most people know nothing of cryptozoology's spectacular scientific success stories. The question one must pose is why do the leftwing secularist academic elites suppress knowledge concerning cryptozoology?

One must first understand that the leftwing academic elites suffer from an extreme form of pessimism. They lack faith in God, but they do not lack faith in Darwin, Marx, or Freud. They

have high IQ's but low levels of common sense.
They understand and believe in the Marxist
dialectic, Freudian psychoanalysis, and
Darwinian macroevolution, but they do not
understand human nature. They cannot
understand anything that contradicts or goes
beyond the methodological naturalism espoused
by Darwin, Marx, and Freud. The prism through
which they view the world is distorted, for it is
based upon false premises and presuppositions.

Their distorted prism causes them to see
truth as falsehood and falsehood as truth. Let me
give you examples of how this effects their
judgement. In 1898, the Director of the U.S.
Patent Office said that the patent office should be
shut down, because "There is nothing more to
invent."

After the fall of the Berlin Wall in 1989 and
after the collapse of the Soviet Union in 1991,
Francis Fukuyama wrote a book entitled *The End
of History*. He predicted that with the intellectual
collapse of Communism and the triumph of
"democracy" and capitalism, history had ended.
All people now would live in peace and harmony
within capitalistic democracies. Conflict over the
great isms had ended. Now everyone could have
peace and happiness through elections and
materialistic goods. Wars would cease. Utopia
would ensue.

How could such a high IQ academic like
Fukuyama be so naive? It happens all the time.
They are naive because they don't understand the
sinful nature of man. Remember, they operate on
the false premise that materialism is all there is.
They think crime is caused by poverty. They

don't realize that crime is caused by sin within the individual, by character flaws. Poverty does not cause character flaws. Today in America character flaws cause poverty. The executives at Enron committed crimes not because they were poor, but because they had character flaws.

A little boy that has to fight the bully on the first day of school during recess on the playground understands human nature better than all the leftwing academic elites combined. The school bully could care less about different "isms". He just enjoys fighting. He enjoys exercising his will over others.

In 1812, French naturalist Georges Cuvier said, "There is little hope of discovering new species of large quadrupeds." (A quadruped is an animal that walks on four feet.) He was just as dead wrong as the director of the patent office who said nothing more could be invented. The truth is there was a lot more to invent and there were many more quadrupeds to be discovered.

Often times the first report of a large quadruped, which has not yet been documented by Western scientists, is put forth by a native in the jungle. Most of the leftwing academic elites are white liberals who summarily dismiss the testimony of a black native in the bush because of their racial bigotry. Deep down they believe that only a white liberal male with a PhD can be trusted.

The leftwing academic elite are very slow to accept reality. They dismissed the first reports of the duck billed platypus, giant squid, mountain gorilla, and Komodo dragon as "hoaxes, delusions, or misidentifications." Today all of these animals are a matter of firm scientific fact.

Ask yourself one question: who should know more about the wildlife in a remote region of the Congo? A native pygmy who has lived there his whole life, hunts there, and hears the oral traditions passed on by his ancestors who have lived there for centuries, or a white liberal academic who lives in an ivory tower on an American university campus?

Finally, one of the most important reasons cryptozoology and its successes are suppressed by the leftwing academic elites is because it has undermined the very foundation of Darwinian macro-evolutionary theory. One of the best examples of this was the discovery of a live coelacanth (pronounced "see-la-kanth") in 1938.

According to the leftwing academic elites, the coelacanth is found in the fossil record at 400 million years old. The oldest coelacanth fossil finds are dated to a time millions of years before the dinosaurs. The coelacanth continues in the fossil record from 400 to 66 million years ago. According to PBS Nova, "After that, they vanish from the fossil record and so were thought to have gone extinct 66 million years ago." The Coelacanth was supposed to have gone extinct with the dinosaurs 66 million years ago. So said the top ranking leftwing academic elites. But they were proven wrong in 1938, when a real live coelacanth was discovered. Many other live coelacanths have been discovered since.

The discovery of the coelacanth has been called "The most important zoological find of the century." It has been called a "living fossil". But what we call it is not as important as its implications. Darwinian macro-evolutionary theory posits that all creatures evolve over millions of years and turn into completely different species. Fish over millions of years turn into apes and apes turn into men. Dinosaurs turn into birds. The coelacanth discoveries demolish this Darwinian macro-evolutionary premise. That is why this success of cryptozoology is suppressed, or when it is broached it is spun away from its true implications.

It is a shame that "The most amazing event of the century in the realm of natural history" is unknown to the average American college graduate. It is time for the truth and its implications to be revealed.

Many leftists, when told about the coelacanth, will try to play it down by stating "well there probably are many species of fish and marine life undocumented by Western science, but as far as large land mammals they were all discovered and documented years ago." This statement is simply false. Just as false as the statement, "There is nothing more to invent."

For example in 1975, Western scientists documented for the first time a living chacoan peccary. It was discovered in South America. Its closest known relative is the pig. It eats "prickly cactus". Chacoan peccaries "remove the spines on the cacti by rolling them around with their rubbery snouts". The interesting fact is that the chacoan peccary is found in the fossil record dated back 37 million years. Like the coelacanth it is a "living fossil" which prior to 1975 was considered to be extinct.

The coelacanth and the chacoan peccary are not the only "living fossils". *U.S. News and World Report* (Oct. 27, 2003, p.73) had an article entitled "Living Fossil." It stated, "Its bulbous body and tiny eyes may not command respect, but this newly discovered species of frog is a survivor. Found in the mountains of Southern India and announced last week in *Nature*, it is a remnant of a group of frog that flourished in the era of dinosaurs." When it comes to the coelacanth, the chacoan peccary, and this newly discovered dino-era frog, Sir Arthur Conan Doyle's *Lost World* fiction seems to ring truer than Charles Darwin's *Origin of the Species*, which was supposed to be a non-fiction book.

At the Cincinnati Zoo I got a chance to see a live Okapi. This animal was unknown to Western science up until 1901. I could hardly believe my eyes. The legs and hindquarters of this animal look like a zebra. The neck and face look like a giraffe. If a child imagined an animal half-zebra/half giraffe, this is what it would look like.

The Okapi has some strange features. It is the "only mammal that can clean its ears with its tongue." Gordy Slack wrote, "with a tongue long enough to lick its own eyes, hind flanks striped like those of a zebra, and hearing so finely honed that it could sense and elude approaching hunters with extraordinary skill, the Okapi epitomized the Congo's biological wonders."

"In 1901, explorer and colonial administrator Sir Harry Johnston," with the help of local pygmies, discovered the Okapi in the Ituri Forest. Herbert Lang wrote, "It was one of the survivors of the giraffine group, such as the paleotragus and helladotherium, flourishing in Southern Asia and Europe during Miocene ages, several million years ago. The okapi had found a safe retreat in the heart of Africa, in the gloom of the Congo Forests." Once again one must ask the question, given millions of years, where was the Darwinian macroevolution from one species to another? The evidence doesn't square with the theory, so they suppress the evidence from the world history and biology textbooks.

The native pygmies in the Congo knew about the Okapi long before Western science acknowledged its existence. The Hmong tribesmen of the Annamite Mountains of Laos on the border of Vietnam have known about many animal species long before Western scientists acknowledged their existence. These "discoveries" of Western science are extremely recent and are ongoing.

In 1992 Western scientists acknowledged the discovery of a large land mammal known as the Saola. It lives in the Annamite Mountains of Laos and Vietnam. Saola is a native term, which means "spindle horn". The Saola's horns "resemble the upright posts of the spindles used in local weaving."

According to www.ultimateungulate.com (ungulate means having hoofs), "The Saola is generally considered to be the greatest animal discovery in recent times, and is so different from any currently known species that a separate genus has had to be constructed." The Saola looks like an ox with two long straight swept back horns. The horns grow to be 20 inches long. The neck looks like that of an antelope. The Saola weights about 200 pounds.

The Saola wasn't "discovered" by Western science until 1992. Many leftwing academics like to preach about mass extinctions taking place today because capitalist industrialists are polluting the earth's environment. The facts do not support the leftwing environmentalist thesis. As George Schaller, the director of science for the Wildlife Conservation Society's international program said, "During the 1990's more species of hoofed animals have been discovered or rediscovered in the Annamite Mountains than are known to have become extinct worldwide in the past few hundred years. These include the Saola, the giant barking deer and what is probably the small rooseveltorum-barking deer, which was first described in 1929 then vanished until it was rediscovered in 1995. Scientists speculate that ice age glaciers during the Pleistocene Epoch affected the distribution of forests upon which species like these depend. Small populations of survivors evolved in isolation in this Noah's Ark lost in time."

The BBC News on July 1, 1999 announced that Western science just discovered the leaf muntjac or leaf deer. The Wildlife Conservation Society claimed that it was the world's smallest deer species. DNA tests proved that this deer was "a species previously unknown to science." It was also discovered in the Annamite Mountains of Southeast Asia.

Colonel John Blashford-Snell, a member of
Great Britain's Scientific Exploration Society, in a
series of expeditions to Nepal in the 1990's
discovered and documented a new species of
elephant. He found two of them. One named
Raja and one named Kansha. What is so amazing
about this new scientific discovery is that these
two elephants, both in size and shape, look like
pre-historic mammoths!

Marc E.W. Miller who traveled to Nepal in
1996 in order to see Colonel Blashford-Snell's
amazing finds with his own eyes said that, "Raja
was absolutely a mammoth in his appearance,
with a slanting rear end, reptilian tail, wide trunk,
small ears, and descending head features. If only
Raja had more hair, I would swear he looked like
a wooly mammoth. The predominant bumps and
domes found in the fossilized remains of
prehistoric elephants thousands and millions of
years ago were very similar to what I was seeing
with my own eyes."

Marc E.W. Miller went on to say that, "The
average height of the Indian Elephant is typically
seven to eight feet to the shoulder." Raja is eleven
and a half feet to the shoulder. The typical
elephant track is 14 to 15 inches across. Raja's
track is twenty-two inches across. But the most
striking difference between these newly
discovered elephants and all other elephants
living today is that Raja and Kansha have two
huge domes on top of their heads. From the side
it looks like they have one huge dome on top of
their heads, but from a frontal view one can see
two huge domes on their heads. These domes are
reminiscent of the mammoth, which is supposed

to have gone extinct thousands of years ago. Ken Ham's publication posed a rhetorical question, "Those who blithely accept evolutionary dating have a problem: What are features found in mammoths which supposedly vanished more than 10,000 years ago doing in animals today? This issue is not being debated in the public schools because this information is being suppressed from the curriculum. The politically correct paradigm appears unassailable when all the evidence against it is suppressed.

On July 3, 2003 the Associated Press put forth an article entitled "Scientists Baffled by Sea Creature". A gigantic sea creature's remains washed ashore on a beach in Chile. Elsa Cabrera, a Chilean scientist, said, "Apparently it is a gigantic octopus or squid but that's just our initial idea, nothing definite." It was essentially a 13-ton "blob" with only one tentacle left. It was 40 feet in length. "Italian and French zoologists have said the Chilean find matches the description of a bizarre specimen found in Florida in 1896 that one scientist at the time named as 'octopus giganteus'." No one yet knows for sure what this creature is. Hopefully, tests that are underway can solve this zoological mystery.

U.S. News and World Report on April 14, 2003 p. 44 had an incredible photograph of a giant squid. The caption read, "Auckland University of Technology researchers with a 330-pound, 16-foot colossal squid found last week and thought to be the largest intact specimen." When it comes to submarines and sea creatures, Jules Verne's imagination was more prescient than Darwin, Marx, and Freud combined.

In August of 2004, *U.S. News and World Report* had a cover issue entitled, "Mysteries of the Oceans: How New Discoveries Under the Seas are Shaping Our Future." Just as there are still more inventions to be invented, there are still more animals to be discovered. In spite of what Francis Fukuyama said, history has not yet ended; it continues unabated.

Norse legend talked about a gigantic squid known to them as the "Kraken." Scientists considered the Kraken to be nothing more than a fictitious myth until corpses of it were discovered. Now the "myth" is considered to be based upon reality. The *Anglo Saxon Chronicles,* one of the oldest surviving books in the world, tells of people fighting "dragons." Chinese legends speak frequently of "dragons." The Bible mentions the word "dragon" on more than one occasion. Could these "dragons" be dinosaurs?

Sir Richard Owen, an anatomist in Great Britain, invented the word "dinosaur" in 1841. Dinosaur comes from deinos and saurus, which is Greek for "terrible lizard." If a man encountered a dinosaur-like creature prior to 1841 A.D. he could not call it a dinosaur because the word did not exist. He would have most likely called it a dragon or a behemoth. The Bible also mentions and describes the word behemoth.

The King James Version of the Bible translated in 1611 states the following in Job 40:15-24. "Behold now behemoth, which I made with thee; he eateth grass as an ox. Lo now his strength is in his loins, and his force is in the navel of his belly. He moveth his tail like a cedar; The sinews of his stones are wrapped together.

His bones are as strong pieces of brass; his bones are like bars of iron. He is the chief of the ways of God: he that made him can make his sword to approach unto him. Surely the mountains bring him forth food, where all the beasts of the field play. He lieth under the shady trees, in the covert of the reed, and fens. The shady trees cover him with their shadow; the willows of the brook compass him about. Behold, he drinketh up a river, and hasteth not: he trusteth that he can draw up Jordan into his mouth. He taketh it with his eyes: his nose pierceth through snares."

Many Bible commentators as well as Bible dictionaries say that the Behemoth mentioned in Job chapter 40 is most likely an elephant or a hippopotamus. This is clearly not the case. For a hippo and an elephant have extremely small tails, and the behemoth has a tail like a cedar tree, which is huge. The description of the Behemoth in Job Chapter 40 fits the description of a sauropod dinosaur like brachiosaurus, much more so than it fits the description of a hippo or elephant, according to Biblical researcher Ken Ham. Sauropod dinosaurs have huge tails the size of cedar trees.

Could a sauropod dinosaur like the behemoth in the Bible be living today in the jungle covered rivers and swamps of the Congo? According to the natives who live around the Likoula swamp/Lake Tele region of the Congo, the answer is yes. The natives call the creature "Mokele Mbembe". The natives claim that mokele mbembe has a long neck, a long tail, and it leaves footprints, which are rounded and have three claws. "The closest known animal that has these characteristics is a saurapod dinosaur."

Dr. Roy Mackal, who is a professor of Biology at the University of Chicago, believes that Mokele Mbembe actually does exist. He explored the area of the Likoula Swamp in 1980 and 1981. He learned some interesting things and came to some startling conclusions.

The natives told Dr. Roy Mackel that Mokele Mbembe was a vegetarian. He did not eat meat. He eats a fruit called "Molombo". Mokele Mbembe killed hippos and elephants if they got near his territory, but he would not eat them. Dr. Mackal said he found footprints that convinced him that not only does Mokele Mbembe exist but that it is indeed a sauropod dinosaur.

When the natives are asked to draw Mokele Mbembe they always draw a sauropod dinosaur. When shown pictures of different animals they always point out the sauropod and say "Mokele Mbembe!" "Mokele Mbembe!" Mokele Mbembe means "one that stops the flow of rivers."

The natives say Mokele Mbembe kills by biting and swinging his tail like a weapon. The pygmies claim they killed a Mokele Mbembe around 1960 and all those who ate of it got sick and died. They thought this was a bad omen, so the surviving pygmies threw the bones back into the swamp.

In 1932 "The world famous zoologist and biologist, Ivan T. Sanderson" and animal-trader Gerald Russel were in a dugout canoe paddling up the river when they encountered what might have been Mokele Mbembe. Sanderson wrote, "I don't know what we saw, but the animal, the monster, burned itself into my retinas. It looked like something that ought to have been dead millions of years ago. As a scientist, I should have been happy, of course, but this encounter was so frightening, so nasty, that I never want to see it again."

Trueauthority.com said that the Likouala Swamp is "55,000 square miles, larger than the entire state of Florida; the government has officially declared it 80% unexplored. To the scientific community this area is as foreign as an entirely new planet."

Does a sauropod dinosaur named Mokele Mbembe actually exist in the Congo? We don't know for sure either way, but we must keep searching for the truth. Native accounts should not just be summarily dismissed; they should be thoroughly investigated.

Prior to 1938 no scientist would have believed natives who claimed to have seen a coelacanth, which was supposed to have been extinct for millions of years. There will always be doubting Thomases.

Most modern day leftwing academics are merely the bankrupt heirs of the Darwinian macro-evolutionary estate. For instance, Professor Richard Dawkins is merely one of many mushrooms on the dunghill of Darwinism.

Living fossils, such as the coelacanth, show a fatal flaw in Darwinian macro-evolutionary theory that states all things evolve into new and distinct species over millions of years. The evidence does not square with the theory. Darwinian macro-evolutionary theory is a bankrupt philosophy.

It may sound fantastic that there might actually be a living dinosaur in a swamp infested area of the Congo, but we should never forget what Shakespeare's Hamlet said to Horatio, for we may want to repeat it to Darwin and his present day disciples, "There are more things in heaven and earth then are dreamt of in your philosophy."

13
The Takla Makan Mummies

*"The discovery of these Caucasian mummies
defies history as we know it."*
– The Discovery Channel

In 1987, Dr. Victor Mair, a scholar of
Chinese literature and language and a professor
at the University of Pennsylvania, stumbled onto
an archeological find of historic proportions. He
was leading a group of Americans through a little
museum in Urumchi, which is a small out of the
way town in the extreme western part of China.
He followed a sign that said "mummy exhibition"
into a dark room. He shined his flashlight on the
3,000-year-old human form in front of him. He
was shocked to his very core. He stared into the
face of the colorfully clothed male mummy. What
he saw was not the face of a mongoloid Han
Chinese type person. What he saw was the face
of a Caucasoid type person that looked eerily
similar to his own brother.

The skin of the mummy's face was "pale
ivory in color with high cheekbones, full lips, and
a long nose." His hair was light and he had a full
beard. Dr. Mair said, "He looked like my brother
Dave sleeping there, and that's what really got
me. I just kept looking at him, looking at his
closed eyes. I couldn't tear myself away. I stayed
in there for several hours. I was supposed to be
leading our group. I just forgot about them for
two or three hours."

In 1979, the Chinese Communist
government ordered massive excavations to begin

in the extreme western part of China in order to build more pipelines and railroads. During these excavations that continued into the 1980's mummified human beings were popping up all over the place. The mummies were extremely well preserved because of the exceedingly dry climate of the Takla Makan Desert. The only problem was that most of the mummies were Caucasian. They dated to over 3,000 years of age. They defied not only the Chinese Communist history books but they also defied the American and European history books.

Many of these mummies found in the Takla Makan Desert of western China have blonde hair. Some of these mummies have red hair. Some of these mummies have full-fledged beards. They have large round eyes, long noses, and high cheekbones. Their skin color looks like that of a modern day white European or American.

The clothing worn by these mummies was also well preserved by the dry climate of the Takla Makan Desert. Elizabeth Wayland Barber, an expert on textiles, wrote that the Takla Makan Mummies wore "brightly colored peculiar plaid twill cloths found previously only in Europe and made by the Celts." Irene Good, an expert on "ancient fibers and textile fabrics" agreed with Barber's assessment after carefully studying the mummies' apparel. Irene Good stated that the Takla Makan mummies clothing was made of wool fibers from European sheep. She said, "They were Western to the very fiber." PBS's Nova in its documentary "The Mysterious Mummies of China" said that these mummies wore "Celtic like tartans". Not only were their faces European but so were their clothes.

Paolo Francalacci, an expert in DNA, from the University of Sassari in Italy, was able to successfully test DNA samples from the mummies of the Takla Makan Desert of western China. The DNA proved that these mummies were of European descent. The faces of the Takla Makan mummies, the apparel of the Takla Makan mummies, and the DNA of the Takla Makan mummies pointed to only one conclusion: these mummies were Celtic Caucasoids.

Libby Rosof wrote in a publication of the University of Pennsylvania that, "The earliest group of mummies, dating from 2000 to 1000 B.C., were not simply Caucasoid. Mair believes they are the ancestors of the Tocharians, a group that spoke an Indo-European language related to Celtic languages." Elizabeth Wayland Barber said that the "Indo-European family tree of languages, when organized by dialect similarity, rather than modern geography, shows Tokharian on the branch next to Celtic. For Tokharian shares more linguistic features with Celtic than with any other branch." Not surprisingly, a handful of important Chinese words have Indo-European etymologies.

Victor Mair, being an expert on ancient Chinese literature and language, realized that many Chinese books and poems told about "tall men with green eyes and red hair". For example the "Song: General Lu" states, "green-eyed general, you well know the will of heaven!" Prior to the discovery of the tall Caucasoid Takla Makan mummies he tried to advance the argument in American academia that these tales of green-eyed men were historically accurate descriptions of Europeans who had entered western China during the Bronze Age. His colleagues in academia scoffed at him and his theory. The conventional wisdom in academia prior to the discovery of the Takla Makan mummies was that these stories of tall green-eyed men with red hair and beards were just false myths, legends, and fairy tales. They had no basis in fact. These new archeological finds vindicate Victor Mair and destroy the conventional wisdom.

Ellen O'Brien, a staff writer for the *Philadelphia Inquirer*, reported, "In an article Mair wrote for *Archaeology* Magazine last year, he, himself, says: 'The new finds are also forcing a reexamination of old Chinese books that describe historical or legendary figures of great height, with deep-set blue or green eyes, long noses, full beards, and red or blond hair. Scholars have traditionally scoffed at these accounts, but it now seems that they may be accurate'." Once again a man who had faith in the myths, the legends, the ancient traditions was proven to be right, while the politically correct doubting Thomases were proven to be wrong.

Why was this find so significant? First, the archeological find of the Takla Makan mummies destroyed the existing historical paradigm. As the *Discovery Channel* said, "The discovery of these Caucasian mummies defy history as we know it." The orthodox historical paradigm was that Chinese culture bloomed in total isolation. No white people were supposed to be in China 3,000 years ago. The history textbooks claim that the first Western contact with China took place 2,000 years ago. The Takla Makan mummies are 1,000 years before their time. PBS's Nova stated, "They radically change our view of a critical time. A European people penetrated China's isolation 1,000 years earlier then previously thought."

Some may still say, ok, Europeans were in China 1,000 years before our history books said they were, so what's the big deal? This brings us back to the linguistic evidence that coincides with the archeological evidence. The Chinese term for "wheel" is the same as the Tokharian word for wheel. Elizabeth Wayland Barber wrote, "The Chinese borrowed a sizable cluster of words to do with wheels and chariots; They encountered a new and highly useful technology among their neighbors and borrowed both the technology and the words connected with it. We know from linguistics that those words came from Indo-European sources, and we know from archaeology that the peculiar art of making spoked wheels (and with them a chariot light enough to be drawn by fleet-footed horses) was developed at the western end of Asia, in the vicinity of the southern Urals, during the third and early second millennia. We know too, that this wave of technology entered China in the mid-second millennium B.C. Such information indicated that the Chinese learned chariotry from speakers of Indo-European languages." The Europeans invented the spoked wheel and chariot, and they introduced it to the Chinese.

The logic is crystal clear. The French word for blue jeans is blue jeans. The Americans invented blue jeans and of course gave it an

English name. The French acquired blue jeans from the Americans, but having no French equivalent of this new invention, they not only borrowed the object but also the name. If the French had invented blue jeans they would have a French name. If the Chinese had invented the spoked wheel, it would have a Chinese name, not an Indo-European name.

PBS Nova stated that, "The mummy people used the wheel long before it was known in China and may have played a role in introducing it to Chinese civilization." This is a bombshell; A smoking gun. For none of the Chinese textbooks, or for that matter the modern Western textbooks, mention this fact. They all state just the opposite. They claim China blossomed on its own, without the help of Western influences. The Chinese invented everything by themselves. The Europeans were just ignorant savages stuck in a dark age. This is the paradigm fiercely favored by the Communists in the Chinese government and their fellow travelers in the American academic establishment. The Communists in the Chinese government and the leftists in the Western academic establishment don't care about the facts; they care only about supporting and defending a paradigm, which they perceive has a therapeutic and political advantage for their ideology. The paradigm which states China developed on its own in isolation makes the Chinese Communists feel good, because they can claim superiority over the West; and it makes the leftists in American academia feel good because they can claim Western inferiority, which salves their guilty conscience for having been descended from (if not genetically, at least culturally, they all speak the Anglo-Saxon language known as English) what they perceive to have been evil Western imperialists. The Chinese Communist leaders are sadistic. The leftists in American academia are masochistic. That is why those two groups support one another and get along so well.

The worst part of this story concerns the suppression of scientific evidence. The PBS Nova documentary *Mysterious Mummies of China* stated, "The Chinese government tried to suppress these archaeological finds." A press release by NOVA/WGBH reported that, "The physical evidence flies in the face of long-held Chinese views that their own civilization developed, independent of outside influences. Consequently, the new discoveries are being downplayed and even suppressed by the present Chinese regime." Dr. Joann Fletcher was quoted by the BBC as saying, "They have Caucasian features, red-blond hair and even Tartan clothing. Their discovery in the Takla Makan Desert in China has understandably caused consternation!" Isn't it amazing that the mummified remains, of a "cow-eyed", Celtic, Caucasoid, could cause such consternation? Unfortunately, these new discoveries have caused so much consternation among the Chinese Communist officials, leftwing American academics, and leftwing American news broadcasters, that all three of these groups have joined in the effort to suppress the inconvenient facts. They have all three joined in the effort to suppress history as it happened.

Libby Rosof of the University of Pennsylvania wrote that, "The Chinese were concerned about the political implications of the discovery out of fear that the local people, the Uyghurs, would use the mummies to prove their long-term residence in the westernmost reaches of China, thereby laying claim to the land." See, the ethnic group that controls China is a group of mongoloids known as the Han. The Han treat the Uyghurs as second-class citizens. The Han consider the Uyghurs evil foreigners in their own country who must be kept under control and not be allowed to gain their independence or freedom. *USA Today* on September 23, 2000 (p.15) said, "Ethnic Uyghurs say their culture is being suppressed by Beijing." Beijing is the capital of Communist China.

Heather Pringle, author of *Mummy Congress*, wrote, "Amnesty International's 1999 report for Xinjiang made grim reading. 'Scores of Uyghurs, many of them political prisoners, have been sentenced to death and executed in the past two years. Others, including women, are alleged to have been killed by the security forces, in circumstances which appear to constitute extra-judicial executions'." The Chinese Communists don't just enjoy killing, imprisoning, and sending off to forced labor camps college students from Tienanmen Square, or Buddhist Monks from Tibet, but they enjoy using these same tactics on Uyghurs in western China as well.

"He who controls the past controls the future." And the Communist Chinese government in Beijing wants to control the future of western China. In order to do so they must control its past. For the Tarim Basin of western China supposedly contains 18 billion tons of crude oil.

Heather Pringle said that this is "six times more than the known reserves of the United States." History is being suppressed for present day political purposes.

One Takla Makan female mummy became known as the "Beauty of Loulan". The Uyghurs disseminated posters, which contained her picture. Pringle writes, "That she was so caucasion-looking was not a problem in Uyghur eyes: some Uyghurs had Caucasian features. People in Urumchi, the province's capital, were captivated. Musicians began writing songs about her that subtly alluded to the separatist cause." The Chinese Communist government decided that this had to be nipped in the bud. If it meant suppressing history, then so be it. The Chinese Communist government would suppress history in order to uphold the politically correct paradigm.

The PBS Nova documentary on the Takla Makan mummies explained how two Communist Chinese officials watched over the scientists. They told the American scientists which graves they could dig up. All the graves looked tampered with. Five of the six were completely empty. One of the six contained a mummy with its head missing. They concluded that the Communist Chinese government did not want the American scientists to see the Caucasoid face of the mummy. They felt the need to suppress.

The geneticist and DNA expert Paolo Francalacci, while in China, collected twenty-five DNA samples from eleven mummies. According to Heater Pringle, "Chinese authorities suddenly demanded Francalacci's samples, refusing to allow them out of the country. Then a mysterious thing happened. Just shortly before Mair departed for home, a Chinese colleague turned up with a surreptitious gift. He slipped five of the confiscated, sealed samples into Mair's pocket. These had come from two mummies. The grateful Mair passed the samples on to Francalacci, who began toiling in Italy to amplify the DNA." Once again the Chinese government tried to suppress the scientific evidence for political reasons.

National Geographic magazine published an article on the Takla Makan mummies in March of 1996. It was written by Thomas B. Allen. It tells a sad story concerning the suppression of scientific evidence. Allen writes, "At Niya, I found a sherd of pottery bearing the fingerprint of the potter. Excited, I showed it to Wang Binghua, Xinjiang's leading archaeologist and an authority on Niya, who was traveling with us. I asked for permission to bring it back to the United States, where I told him a forensic anthropologist might be able to extract information about the potter by studying the fingerprint. Wang Binghua, a Han Chinese, held the pottery for a moment, then asked: 'Would he be able to tell if the potter was a white man?' I said I didn't know. He nodded and put the sherd in his pocket. I never saw it again."

Science is supposed to be a search for the truth. But today, if scientific evidence is discovered which goes against one of the prevailing politically correct paradigms, it is immediately suppressed by the leftists in the media and academia. Dan Rather of CBS news will trumpet newly discovered forged documents in an attempt to destroy the re-election of George W. Bush, but he will not trumpet newly discovered scientific evidence, which pulverizes a politically correct paradigm. Watching the *CBS* evening news, I have not heard them mention the Takla Makan Mummies. Reading Prentice Hall's *World History* textbook: *Connections to Today*, published in 2001, I can find no mention of the Takla Makan Mummies. The leftists in the media and academia have felt the need to suppress an archeological find of historic proportions.

Elizabeth Wayland Barber, author of *The Mummies of Urumchi*, wrote concerning the Tokharian caucasoids bringing the spoked wheel, chariots, and bronze swords into western China over 3,000 years ago, "Some have tried to wish away the evidence for such transcontinental contacts, believing that independent invention confers the greatest glory." The leftists want to "wish away" the truth.

Victor Mair realizes that leftists in the American media and academia suffer from a guilt complex. They believe that by suppressing history, they can salve their guilty conscience. Victor Mair said, "There's a lot of Western guilt about imperialism and sensitivity about dominating other people. It's a really deep subconscious thing, and there are a lot of people in the West who are hypersensitive about saying our culture is superior in any way, or that our culture gets around or extends itself."

Muslim terrorists have only one thing in common with American leftwing liberals. They both hate America and the Western Civilization it represents. Muslim terrorists hate America and the West because they are jealous of its accomplishments. American leftwing intellectuals hate America and the West because they feel guilty about its accomplishments. This is the psychological phenomenon that binds together these two disparate groups in a common cause: The destruction of America from within as well as from without.

14
Conclusion – The Good Fight

"He who controls the past, controls the future."
– George Orwell

The liberals in the media and academia suppressed crucial facts concerning the historical events that led up to 9-11. Jack Cashill of *World Net Daily* has laid bare many of these pieces of the puzzle that were suppressed by the "mainstream" news media.

For example, many facts were suppressed concerning the Oklahoma City bombing of the Murrah Federal Building. For instance, Terry Nichols may have met with Ramzi Yousef in the Philippines just prior to the blowing up the Murrah Federal Building in Oklahoma City. Ramzi Yousef was the Muslim terrorist who bombed the World Trade Center in 1993. Richard Clarke in his book *Against All Enemies*, wrote, "We do know that Nichols' bombs did not work before his Philippine stay and were deadly when he returned."

When Yousef and Nichols were in the Philippines at the same time in November, December, and January of 1995, Philipino police raided Yousef's apartment. They found Yousef's lap top computer and Abdul Hakim Murad. Murad revealed their plans for "Operation Bojinka," which entailed hijacking commercial airliners and crashing them into American targets. Cashill writes, "The Philippine police even make a flow chart connecting many of the key players together, including Osama Bin Laden, Ramzi Yousef and 9-11 mastermind Khalid Shaikh Mohammed, Yousef's uncle. Philippine authorities turned over all of this information to U.S. authorities by early 1995." The Clinton administration suppressed this information, because Clinton did not want to engage in a Middle Eastern war and throw a monkey wrench into his re-election plans for 1996. He was already ahead in the polls. The economy was good. He would do everything in his power to play down the threat of Islamic terrorism, so that he would not be forced into going to war. Clinton's personal need to be reelected took precedence over America's need to be protected.

Jayna Davis in her book *The Third Terrorist* documents over 20 reliable eyewitnesses who saw Timothy McVeigh, Terry Nichols' best friend, with a Middle Eastern looking man. This man became known to the world as John Doe #2. McVeigh was seen in Oklahoma City with a swarthy looking short Middle Eastern man in a yellow Ryder truck just prior to the bombing. The testimony of these witnesses was suppressed. John Doe #2 was suppressed. Clinton was able to shift the blame for the Oklahoma City bombing away from Middle Eastern terrorists and pin it solely on two "Lily white" individuals, McVeigh and Nichols. This allowed the Democratic strategists to attack the influence of Rush Limbaugh and Newt Gingrich, whom the Clinton strategists blamed as ideological co-conspirators in the Oklahoma City Bombing. This would help to paint white conservative males as evil and pave the way for Clinton's successful re-election bid.

Muslim terrorists used another truck bomb to kill Americans at the Khobar Towers in Saudi Arabia on June 25, 1996. Clinton treated this as a low-level law enforcement nuisance, not as an act of war against America.

On July 17, 1996 TWA Flight 800 blows up in mid-air off the coast of Long Island. 270 highly educated witnesses saw a missile zooming through the air impacting the plane. Federal Aviation Administration radar operators in New York "saw on their screen an unknown object 'merging' with TWA 800 in the seconds before the crash and rushed the radar data to Washington." FBI agents early on told the *New York Times* "that explosive residue has been found throughout the plane and especially along the right wing. The FBI's Washington Lab has identified the residue as PETN, a component of either missiles or bombs. The same *New York Times* article calls the finding 'a serious blow to the already remote possibility that a mechanical accident caused the crash'."

On August 22, 1996, Jamie Gorelick, Clinton's deputy Attorney General, Field Commander of the Oklahoma City Investigation, and future 9-11 Commissioner (known for her creation of the wall of separation between the FBI and CIA) ordered Jim Kallstrom head of the National Transportation Safety Board's investigation of Flight 800 to meet with her in Washington D.C. After that meeting all top government officials in the Clinton White House, as well as Kallstrom, put forth unequivocally the conclusion that TWA Flight 800 had a mechanical problem with its fuel tank and that was why it exploded. Once again, Middle Eastern terrorism was played down, covered up, and suppressed, so that Bill Clinton could win reelection without a messy Middle Eastern war on his hands. Bill Clinton always believed more in himself then he did in America. Clinton subordinated America's national security for his own selfish ambitions.

On October 3, 2004, the *History Channel* aired a documentary on TWA Flight 800. Jack Cashill writes "Producer Bob Schneiger closed [the documentary] with the observation that the FAA made no effort to address the alleged fuel tank problem for eight years, but spent a billion immediately on beefed up airport security."

Also in 1996, someone planted a bomb, which blew up in Atlanta, Georgia during the Olympic games. This is known as the Olympic Park Bombing. The Clinton Administration blamed Richard Jewell, a "Lily white" American male, who was actually a hero who saved many peoples lives. The FBI hounded Richard Jewell for months until after Clinton was reelected. After Clinton was reelected, the FBI released a statement that Jewell did not plant the bomb. They let him be. The bomber was never located.

Jack Cashill of *World Net Daily* believes a Muslim terrorist probably planted this bomb. For El-Sayyid Nosair in 1990 "blew up a 'gay' bar in Greenwich Village." But, of course the Clinton Administration wanted to blame the Atlanta Olympic park bombing on a "Lily white" American male, for it would be politically incorrect to blame it on a Muslim terrorist. First they tried to blame it on Richard Jewell. When they knew they had not one shred of evidence that Jewell did it, they turned the blame onto Eric Rudolph. The political correctness movement dictates that liberals must never blame Muslim terrorists for any wrongdoing if at all possible. If it is not possible, then at least sympathize with the Muslim terrorists and blame the American and Israeli policies for having been the root cause of the terrorist action. Remember, the National Education Association's website implored teachers after 9-11 not to place blame for the destruction of the World Trade Center on any one particular group.

American leftists in the government, the media, and academia suffer from a masochistic guilt complex. That is why they ally themselves with America's enemies. During the Cold War they allied themselves with Communists and fought against President Reagan's anti-Communist initiatives such as aiding the Contra Freedom Fighters in Central America. Today, during the war on terrorism, they ally themselves with the terrorists and fight against Bush's initiatives to kill Muslim terrorists in the Middle East. As Jeanne Kirkpatrick said, "They blame America first."

A perfect example of this leftwing masochism of the academic and political left was when Columbia professor Nicholas De Genova said, "The only true heroes are those who find ways that help defeat the U.S. military...I personally would like to see a million Mogadishus." Deep down, the political left hates not only the U.S. military but also America herself.

The Democrat party under the leadership of Clinton and Gore gave the Communist Chinese "sensitive weapons technology" in exchange for campaign cash. Al Gore even picked up a $100,000 check from a Buddhist Monk in a monastery, even though Monks are supposed to have taken a vow of poverty. China now controls the company that controls the Panama Canal, which Jimmy Carter gave away. China has forced the Internet search engine Google to bow to political censorship of many sites in China, according to *CNN.com* article "Google Bows to Chinese Censorship" (September 27, 2004).

Lev Navrozov of *Newsmax.com* says that China is spending vast sums of money in an attempt to develop NANO weapons. This is the use of nanotechnology to make weapons of mass destruction. According to Navrozov, they are far ahead of America in the realm of nano-weapons. He says that allowing Communist China to develop nano-weapons before the United States does would be akin to allowing Nazi Germany to develop the nuclear bomb prior to the United States developing it. In other words, it would lead to disaster on a grand scale. It could lead to the total defeat of the United States.

The liberals in the media and academia suppress all of this information. For it is not politically correct to portray Muslims or Communists as villains. Even the Muslim terrorists in a Tom Clancy novel entitled *The Sum Of All Fears* had to be changed into Lily-white males by the Hollywood elite before the film could be released.

Two Communist Chinese Colonels wrote a book entitled *Unrestricted Warfare* in which they wrote, "Whether it be the intrusions of hackers, a major explosion at the World Trade Center, or a bombing attack by Bin Laden, all of these greatly exceed the frequency bandwidths understood by the American military." The problem is they wrote this three years before the 9-11-01 attack on the World Trade Center's twin towers in New York City. The authors Colonel Qiao Liang and Colonel Wang Xiangsui "have been hailed as heroes in China since September 11," so says Newsmax.com. Admiral Thomas Moorer, the former Chairman of the Joint Chiefs of Staff said, "You need to read *Unrestricted Warfare* because it reveals China's game plan in its coming war with America...China thinks it can destroy America by using these tactics." The liberals in the media and academia have suppressed all of this information.

Culturally speaking, Charles Dickens was right; we live in the best of times and the worst of times, all at the same time. We live in an age of good and evil. We live in an age with the *The Passion of The Christ* and the *Last Temptation of Christ*. We live in an age of J.R.R. Tolkien and Michael Moore. We live in an age of Pat Tillman and John Walker Lindh. We live in an age of the *Left Behind Series* and the *DaVinci Code*. We live in an age of adult stem cell research and embryonic stem cell research. We live in an age of traditional marriage and same sex marriage. We live in a time when good is juxtaposed next to evil.

What's in fashion today in America's history departments within the hallowed halls of academia is "political correctness." It may be what's in fashion, but it does not teach what is important. As President Ronald Reagan said in his farewell address, "So we've got to teach history based not on what's in fashion, but what's important." President Reagan, in that same speech, warned us against the "eradication of the American memory".

We must reveal the truth about history as it actually happened. We must reveal the truth about military history such as Custer's Last Stand, and the lessons of the Tet Offensive; Political history such as Immigration and Islamic terrorism; Social History such as dress, music, and art, and Natural History such as the Takla Makan Mummies and Noah's Flood.

We must succeed in our mission to do this, for as George Orwell said, "He who controls the past controls the future." Unfortunately, today our past is controlled by the academic and political left. They write most of the history textbooks, make most of the movies, and report most of the news. They are starting to lose their control and their credibility because of talk radio, the Internet, and *Fox* news. These 3 entities are chipping away at the visible portion of the leftist iceberg. The visible portion of the iceberg is represented by current events. The non-visible portion of the iceberg, the part below the surface of the water, is represented by history. We must destroy the entire iceberg, so that our ship of state can sail safe and free into the future and not meet the fate of the *Titanic*. It will take passionate intensity from a few good men in order to save our nation-state from the masochistic impulses of the political and academic left. For it is the leftists who make us vulnerable to attacks from our Islamo-Fascist and Communist enemies.

Leftwing professors want to brainwash our children. Rock and rap stars want to degrade our children. Islamic terrorists want to kill our children. Liberals want to convince us to euthanize our grandparents and to abort our babies. This type of evil must be identified and defeated.

A cultural war is being waged. We must get off the sidelines and enter the fray. We must engage. Like Maverick in *Top Gun* we must enter the fight before it is too late.

Rudyard Kipling understood that we must enter the race before we can finish the course. As he said, we must "fill the unforgiving minute with 60 seconds worth of distance run."

In the end, when we die and meet our Maker, I hope that we will all be able to honestly say what Paul said in the scriptures, "I fought the good fight, I finished the course, I kept the faith."

Bibliography

Chapter 1

Abraham, Priya. "Remembering Rwanda." *World*, April 24, 2004. p. 25-27

Balakian, Peter. *The Burning Tigris: The Armenian Genocide and America's Response.* New York: Harper Collins, 2003.

Bartlett, Bruce. "The Diversity Colleges Lack: Survey Confirms Faculties Overwhelmingly Liberal." *Human Events*, 2004.

Bluey, Robert. "ABC's Stossel Rips Network for Hostility to Conservatives." *CNSNews.com*, January 28, 2004.

Dawson, John. "Painfully Unaware." *World*, April 24, 2004. p. 24

Duin, Julia. "Mel Gibson Looks Right for Movie on Jesus." *The Washington Times*, July 6, 2003.

Farah, Joseph. "Rape Gangs Target Whites-Racial Violence Surges in Zimbabwe." *WorldNetDaily.com*, Feb. 9, 2004.

Gavel, Doug. "Belfer Center Associate Holds Ground in Genocide Debate." *The Harvard University Gazette*, Oct. 12, 2000.

Goldberg, Bernard. "Ever Notice Liberal Bias?" *Wall Street Journal*, June 12, 2002. p. A18

Hardy, Quentin. "Hitting Slavery Where it Hurts." *Forbes*, Jan. 12, 2004. p. 76-78

Kimball, Roger. "Academia vs. America." The *American Legion Magazine*, April 2003. p. 34-38

Lacey, Marc. "Panel Led by U.S. Criticizes
Sudan's Government Over Slavery." *New
York Times*, May 23, 2004. p. A.17

Limbaugh, Rush. "Mel Gibson: The Rush
Profile." *The Limbaugh Letter*, Dec. 2003.

Vlahos, Kelley. "Colorado State Senator Attacks
University Bias." *www.foxnews.com*, Jan.
19, 2004.

www.historywiz.org/annihilation.htm. "Adolf
Hitler and the Annihilation of the
Armenians." Jan. 13, 2004.

Chapter 2

Bohrer, Becky. "Other Side of the Story Now at
Little Bighorn Site." *Cincinnati Enquirer*.
June 26, 2003.

Curry, Andrew. "Custer's Bluster: His
Courageous Last Stand may be a Figment."
U.S. News and World Report-Mysteries of
History-Special Collector's Edition. 2001.
p. 31-32. (also published in the 7-24-00
issue of *USN and WR*)

Fialka, John J. "Amid Victory Cries at Little
Bighorn, a Few Tears for Custer." *Wall
Street Journal*. June 25, 2003.

Fox, Richard. "Unsolved History: Custer's Last
Stand." *The Discovery Channel*. Nov. 6,
2002. (Documentary)

Goodman, Rebecca. "Ohio Moments: George A.
Custer was Brash, Bold, and Heroic."
Cincinnati Enquirer. June 25, 2003. p. B2

Hutton, Paul Andrew. "Live Chat: Custer's Last
Stand-with Custer Scholar Paul Hutton."
Transcript of interview-chat-mysteries of

History-U.S. News online.
*www.usnews.com/usnews/doubleissue/m
ysteries/chat.html.* Dec. 30, 2003.
Keogh, M.W. "The Custer Clan: General: Mwkeogh
vs. Dr. Richard Fox."
*groups.msn.com/TheCusterClan/general.ms
nw? action.* Sep. 3, 2003.
Streissguth, Thomas. *Custer's Last Stand:
Opposing Viewpoints Series-At Issue in
History.* New York: Greenhaven Press,
2003.
Utley, Robert M. *George Armstrong Custer and
the Western Military Frontier.* Norman
Oklahoma: University of Oklahoma Press,
2001. p. 190 and p. 168

Chapter 3

Goldstein, Donald. *At Dawn We Slept Afterword.*
New York: Viking Penguin Inc., 1991.
Hart, B.H. Liddell. *History of the Second World
War.* New York: G.P. Putnam's Sons,
1971.
Keegan, John. *The Price of Admiralty: The
Evolution of Naval Warfare.* New York:
Viking Penguin Inc., 1988.
Prange, Gordon. *At Dawn We Slept: The Untold
Story of Pearl Harbor.* New York: Viking
Penguin Inc., 1981.
Stinnett, Robert. *Day of Deceit: The Truth About
FDR and Pearl Harbor.* New York: Simon
and Schuster, 2001.
Toland, John. *Infamy: Pearl Harbor and Its
Aftermath.* New York: Doubleday, 1983.

www.history.navy.mil/faqs/faq66-9.htm. "The Pearl Harbor Attack, 7 December 1941: Where were the Carriers, 7 December 1941?" August 19, 2003.

Chapter 4

Dupuy, Ernest. *The Encyclopedia of Military History.* Harper and Row: New York, 1986, p. 1337.

Johnson, Haynes. *The Bay of Pigs.* New York: W.W. Norton and Company, Inc., 1964

Kohn, George C. *Dictionary of Wars.* Anchor Press Doubleday, Garden City, New York, 1987, p. 51, 52.

Kornbluh, Peter. *Bay of Pigs Declassified: The Secret CIA Report on the Invasion of Cuba.* New York: The New Press, 1998.

Lynch, Grayston L. *Decision for Disaster: Betrayal at the Bay of Pigs.* Washington D.C./London: Brassey's Inc., 1998.

Merit Students Encyclopedia. New York: MacMillan Educational Company. 1986, pg. 370.

Peterzell, Jay. "New Look at an Old Failure." *Time.* June 1, 1987. p. 29

Skelly, Jack. "Ducking the Blame at the Bay of Pigs." *www.insightmag.com.* Washington, D.C., Vol. 15, No. 15. April 26, 1999.

Smith, Michael. "The Cuban Disaster." *Time.* April 28, 1961, p. 21.

Triay, Victor A. *Bay of Pigs: An Oral History of Brigade 2506.* Miami: University Press of Florida, 2001.

Wyden, Peter. *Bay of Pigs: The Untold Story.* New York: Simon and Schuster, 1979.

Chapter 5

Braestrup, Peter. *Big Story: How the American Press and Television Reported and Interpreted the Crisis of Tet 1968 in Vietnam and Washington.* New York: Doubleday, 1978.

Coulter, Ann. "Tit for Tet." *WorldNetDaily.com.* May 26, 2004.

Graves, Jim. "Tangled Web: The Vietnam War-An Overview of the Conflict in Southeast Asia." *Soldier of Fortune.* July, 1980.

Hanson, Victor Davis. *Carnage and Culture.* New York: Doubleday Books, 2001.

http://en.wikipedia.org/wiki/tet_offensive. "Tet Offensive". May 30, 2004.

http://prapmatist.mcasuredvoices.com/index.cgi/ books/big_story.html? "The Big Story". Nov. 5, 2003.

McColl, Alexander. "Epilogue and Aftermath: Vietnam as History-SOF Looks Back on How the War Changed the World." *Soldier of Fortune-Back to Battle Vietnam.* Feb. 1986.

Poos, Bob. "Nam: Across the Pond and Into the bush, America Fights its Longest War". *Soldier of Fortune-Back to Battle Vietnam.* Feb. 1986.

Summers, Harry G. *Vietnam War Almanac.* New York: Facts on File Publications, 1985.

Chapter 6

Beecroft, John. *Kipling: A Selection of His Stories and Poems*. Garden City, New York: Doubleday and Co. Inc., 1956. p. 504

Faria, Miguel. "Great Britain and Gun Control: With Neither Liberty Nor Safety." *Newsmax.com*. September 8, 2003.

Johnson, Paul. "Britain: A Thieves' Paradise." *Forbes*. February 17, 2003. p. 35

Kopel, David. *The Samurai, The Mountie, and The Cowboy: Should America Adopt The Gun Controls of Other Democracies?* Buffalo, New York: Prometheus Books, 1992.

Lapierre, Wayne. *Guns Freedom and Terrorism*. Nashville: Thomas Nelson Inc, 2003.

Malcolm, Joyce. "Gun Control's Twisted Outcome. Restricting Firearms has Helped Make England More Crime-ridden than the U.S." *www.reason.com*. November, 2002.

Chapter 7

Barlett, Donald L. "Who Left the Door Open." *Time*. September 20, 2004. p. 51-66

Brimelow, Peter. *Alien Nation*. New York: Random House, 1995.

Buchanan, Patrick J. *The Death of the West*. New York: St. Martin's Press, 2002.

Cook, R.J. *One Hundred and One Famous Poems*. Chicago: The Cable Company, 1924, p. 158, 159

Farah, Joseph. "Al-Qaida South of the Border." *http://www.worldnetdaily.com*. February 16, 2004.

Hanson, Victor Davis. *Mexifornia.* San Francisco: Encounter Books, 2003.

"Honduran Official: Al-Qaida Recruits Central American Gangs." *Newsmax.com Wires.* October 21, 2004.

Lamm, Richard. *The Immigration Time Bomb.* New York: E.P. Dutton, 1985.

Leo, John. "Citizenship on the Cheap." *U.S. News and World Report.* September 22, 2003. p. 31

Leo, John. "More Immigration Folly." *U.S. News and World Report.* January 19, 2004. p. 71

Malkin, Michelle. *Invasion.* Washington, D.C.: Regnery, 2002.

Moore, Roger. "The War on Our Southern Border." *http://www.military.com.* August 18, 2003.

Parker, Randall. "Illegal Alien Border Crossing Surge Seen as Terrorism Threat." *http://www.parapundit.com.* May 18, 2004.

Schlafly, Phyllis. "Lawlessness on the Border." *Human Events.* April 26, 2004.

Spencer, Robert. *Islam Unveiled.* San Francisco: Encounter Books, 2002.

Spencer, Robert. *Onward Muslim Soldiers.* Washington D.C.: Regnery, 2003.

Thomas, Cal. "Islam's Teachings Not All Peaceful." *Cincinnati Enquirer.* October 7, 2001.

Veith, Gene Edward. "Crime as Redemption." *World,* June 19, 2004. p. 35

Vincent, Lynn. "Leaving the Back Door Open." *World.* September 4, 2004. p. 26-27

Zuckerman, Mortimer. "Comparative
Advantages." *U.S. News and World Report.*
August 2, 2004. p. 87-88

Chapter 8

Babwin, Don. "Cosby has Harsh Words for Black
Community." *news.yahoo.com.* July 2,
2004.
Bennett, William J. *The Index of Leading Cultural
Indicators.* New York: Simon and
Schuster, 1994.
Boteach, Shmuley. "The Disgusting Super Bowl
Halftime Show." *worldnetdaily.com.*
February 2, 2004.
Brooks, David. *Bobos in Paradise.* New York:
Simon and Schuster, 2000.
Brooks, David. *On Paradise Drive.* New York:
Simon and Schuster, 2004.
Clark, Kim. "Trash TV: Will Super Bowl Sleaze
Prompt a Real Crackdown on all That Media
Smut?" *U.S. News and World Report.*
February 16, 2004. p. 48-52
Colson, Charles. "Bankrupt at Age Twenty-Five:
Marketing to Teens, Tweens, and Kids."
Breakpoint with Charles Colson.
www.freerepublic.com. August 31, 2004.
Cosby, Bill. "Bill Cosby has more Harsh Words
for Blacks." *Newsmax.com Wires.* July 2,
2004.
Cousins, Norman. "The Decline of Neatness."
Time. April 2, 1990.
Crouch, Stanley. "Hip Hop's Thugs Hit New Low."
Cincinnati Enquirer. August 14, 2003.
p. c-10

Dahl, Richard. "Burned Out and Bored." *Newsweek.* December 15, 1997.

Kovacs, Joe. "Trick or Treat 2004: Pimp and Ho Kids." *worldnetdaily.com.* August 25, 2004.

Kupelian, David. "The Marketing of Evil: Selling Sex and Corruption to Your Kids." *worldnetdaily.com.* January 15, 2004.

Leo, John. "Dennis the Day-Glo Icon." *U.S. News and World Report.* February 3, 1997.

Leo, John. "He Shook up Manhattan." *U.S. News and World Report.* January 14, 2002. p. 47.

Leo, John. "Splitting Society, not Hairs." *U.S. News and World Report.* December 15, 2003.

Leo, John. "The Selling of Rebellion." *U.S. News and World Report.* October 12, 1998.

Malkin, Michelle. "Decency Takes a Stand: Modesty in a Culture of Excess." *The Washington Times* – National Weekly Edition. August 9-15, 2004. p.4

McWhorter, John. *Doing Our Own Thing: The Degradation of Language and Music.* New York: Gotham Books, 2003.

Parker, Kathleen. "Everybody's Doing It." *Jewish World Review.* May 23, 2001.

Prager, Dennis. "One Man Wore Jacket and Tie at High-School Graduation." *worldnetdaily.com.* June 1, 2004.

Schlafly, Phyllis. "Another CBS Travesty." *Human Events.* February 9, 2004. p. 28

Sowell, Thomas. "Elite Make Statements Through Mascots." *Knoxville News-Sentinel.* March 5, 1994.

Veith, Gene Edward. "Clearing the Air." *World*.
February 8, 2003. p. 11

Veith, Gene Edward. "Secure or Spoiled." *World*.
September 13, 2003. p. 8

Wells, Melanie. "Meet Your New Sales Force."
Forbes. February 2, 2004.

Chapter 9

Belz, Joel. "Bad to Worse." *World*. May 29,
2004. p. 8

Belz, Joel. "Christian Pirates." *World*. May 8,
2004. p. 8

Bloom, Allan. *The Closing of the American Mind*.
New York. Simon and Schuster, 1987.

Bronson, Peter. "Next Generation of Churches is
Alive in Vineyard." *Cincinnati-Enquirer*.
Aug. 10, 2003.

CNN.com. "The Music of War: VH1 Chronicles
soldiers and Their Soundtracks." August
17, 2004.

Collins, Bob. "Creed and Prejudice." The
American Spectator. Aug/Sep. 2003. p. 72

Colson, Charles. *How Now Shall We Live*.
Wheaton, IL: Tyndale House Publishers,
1999.

Foust, Michael. "Shallow Choruses Have
Replaced Scriptural Hymns, Panelists Say."
www.worthynews.com. September 8,
2003.

Hamilton, Michael S. "The Triumph of the Praise
Songs: How Guitars Beat out the Organ in
the Worship Wars." *Christianity Today*.
July 12, 1999. www.christianitytoday.com

Karlgaard, Rich. "The Age of Meaning." *Forbes.* April 26, 2004. p. 31.

Kirchheimer, Sid. "Does Rap Put Teens at Risk?" *WebMD Medical News Archive.* March 3, 2003. my.webmd.com

Lemen, Pat. "Modern Worship Like Rock Concert." *Cincinnati Enquirer.* July 27, 2003.

Marsh, Ann. "Can You Hum Your Way to Math Genius?" *Forbes.* April 19, 1999. p. 176-180

McWhorter, John. *Doing Our Own Thing: The Degradation of Language and Music.* New York, Penguin Group, 2003.

Plato. *The Republic.* New York, E.P. Dutton and Co. Inc. 1948.

Samuels, Allison. "Battle for the Soul of Hip-Hop." *Newsweek.* October 9, 2000

Tolson, Jay. "Forget Politics: It's About the Music." *U.S. News and World Report.* April 19, 2004. p. 72-73

Veith, Gene Edward. "God is Interested in Excellence." *World.* July 31, 2004. p. 31.

Veith, Gene Edward. "Pop-Culture Recession." *World.* January 25, 2003. p. 11

Veith, Gene Edward. "Rocking-Chair Rockers." *World.* February 1, 2003. p. 13.

Veith, Gene Edward. "Sick Unto Death: Attacks From Without are Not the Worst Kind of Terrorism." *World.* April 17, 2004. p. 27

Warren, Rick. *The Purpose Driven Life.* Grand Rapids, Michigan: Zondervan, 2002.

Chapter 10

"Piss Christ."
*http://encyclopedia.thefreedictionary.com/p
iss%20Christ.* 8/9/2004.

Clark, Kenneth. *Civilisation.* New York: Harper
and Row, 1969.

Cowley, Geoffrey. "The Biology of Beauty."
Newsweek. June 3, 1996. p. 61-66

Gombrich, Ernst. "The Tyranny of Abstract Art."
Atlantic Monthly. April, 1958. p. 43-48

Hughes, Robert. *The Shock of the New.* New
York: Alfred A. Knopf, 1991.

Johnson, Paul. *Art: A New History.* New York:
Harper Collins, 2003.

Kimball, Roger. "Farewell Mapplethorpe, Hello
Shakespeare." *National Review* on line.
January 29, 2004.
www.nationalreview.com.

Kimball, Roger. *Against the Grain.* Chicago: Ivan
R. Dee, 1995.

Kramer, Hilton. *The New Criterion Reader.* New
York: Macmillan, 1988.

Lazzaroni, Rita. "Did a Car Hit It – Or Maybe a
Train?" *Newsweek.* May 1, 2000. p. 10

Murray, Charles. *Human Accomplishment.* New
York: Harper Collins, 2003.

Papini, Giovanni. New Gogs Diary.
*www.southernoregonartschool.com/whatisa
rt.htm.*

Papini, Giovanni. *The Black Book.* Florence,
Italy: Vallecchi.

Veith, Gene Edward. "A Poet Who Rhymes."
World. November 9, 2002. p. 13

Veith, Gene Edward. "Art For the Red States."
World. June 28, 2003. p. 13

Veith, Gene Edward. "Lights Out in an Empty
Room." *World.* April 13, 2002. p. 11

Chapter 11

"The Antikythera Mechanism: A True Mystery of
the Ancient World."
*http://homepage.mac.com/casewright/essa
ys/antikythera.html*

"The Baghdad Battery." *http://www.world-
mysteries.com/sar_11.htm.* Feb. 24, 2004.

"The Clockwork Computer." *The Economist.*
September 19, 2002. www.economist.com

Burr, Chandler. "The Geophysics of God: A
Scientist Embraces Plate Tectonics – and
Noah's Flood." *U.S. News and World
Report.* June 16, 1997. p. 55-58

Curry, Andrew. "Barbarians Get Sophisticated."
U.S. News and World Report. November 24,
2003. p. 62

Hancock, Graham. *Underworld: The Mysterious
Origins of Civilization.* New York: Crown
Publishers, 2002.

Pitman, Walter and Ryan, William. *Noah's Flood:
The New Scientific Discoveries About the
Event that Changed History.* New York:
Simon and Schuster, 2000.

Price, Derek J. de Solla. "An Ancient Greek
Computer." *Scientific American.* June
1959. p. 60-67

Wilson, Ian. *Before the Flood: The Biblical Flood
as a Real Event and How It Changed the*

Course of Civilization. New York: St.
Martin's Press, 2001.

Chapter 12

"Australian Museum Fish Site: Find a Fish:
Coelacanth."
http://www.dinofish.com/sa_canth.html.
2001.
"BBC News: Sci/Tech: Leaf Deer Takes a Bow."
http://news.bbc.co.uk.1/hi/sci/tech/38290
0.stm. July 1, 1999.
"Chacoan Peccary." *www.greenapple.com.* 2004.
"Chacoan Peccary." *www.stlzoo.org.*
"Chileans to Send 'Blob' Samples to Foreign
Labs." *Reuters.* July 3, 2003.
"Colossal Squid." *U.S. News and World Report.*
April 14, 2003. p.44
"Cryptozoology: From Wikipedia, the Free
Encyclopedia."
http://en.wikipedia.org/wiki/cryptozoology
May 9, 2004.
"Did You Know." *www.danger-*
island.com/true/Mokapi/okapi.html. 2000.
"Discovery of the Coelacanth."
www.dinofish.com. 2002.
"Discovery of the New South African
Coelacanths." *www.dinofish.com.* 2002.
"Living Fossil." *U.S. News and World Report.* Oct.
27, 2003. p. 73
"Mokele Mbembe of Africa."
www.trueauthority.com/cryptozoology/mok
ele.htm. 2002.
"Mokele Mbembe: Overview."
www.mokelembembe.com. 2004.

"Mysteries of the Oceans." *U.S. News and World Report.* Aug. 16-23, 2004.

"Nova: Ancient Creature of the Deep/Anatomy of the Coelacanth/PBS." *http://www.pbs.org/wgbh/nova/fish/anatomy.html.* 2003

"Okapi". *www.colszoo.org.* 2004.

"Pseudoryx Nghetinhensis: Saola." *www.ultimateungulate.com.* 2004.

"Scientists Baffled by Sea Creature." *The Associated Press.* July 3, 2003.

"The Fish Out of Time." *www.parascope.com/en/cryptozoo/predators07.htm.* 2002.

"World's Smallest Deer Species Discovered by Wildlife Conservation Society." *www.sciencedaily.com.* July 6, 1999.

Bille, Matthew A. *Rumors of Existence.* Blaine, WA: Hancock House, 1995.

Blashford-Snell. *Mammoth Hunt: In Search of the Giant Elephants of Nepal.* New York, Harper Collins, 1997.

Gibbons, William. "Was a Mokele Mbembe Killed at Lake Tele?" *www.anomalist.com/reports/mokele.html.* 2002.

Gould, Dr. G.C. "Platygonus". *www.flmnh.ufl.edu/fossilhall/library/peccary/peccary.htm.* 2003.

Ham, Ken. *The Great Dinosaur Mystery Solved.* Green Forest, AR: Master Books, 2000.

Holy Bible: King James Version. Nashville: Thomas Nelson, 1989.

Marvels and Mysteries of Our Animal World:
    Readers Digest. New York: Reader's Digest
    Association, 1979.
McCarthy, Wil. "Lab Notes: Cryptozoology and
    the Aliens of Earth."
    *http://www.scifi.com/sfw/issue127/labnot
    es.html.* 2003.
Miller, Marc E.W. *The Legends Continue:
    Adventure in Cryptozoology.* Kempton, IL:
    Adventures Unlimited, 1998.
Norman, Scott T. "Cryptozoological Realms:
    Mokele Mbembe."
    www.mokelembembe.com. 2002.
Schaller, George. "On the Trail of New Species:
    Annamite Mountains of Laos Yeilds
    Previously Unknown Large Mammal
    Species." *www.findarticles.com.* 2000
Slack, Gordy. "The Elusive Okapi."
    *http://diglib1.amnh.org/articles/Okapi/Ok
    api1.htm.* 2004.
Wieland, Carl. "Lost World Animals Found!"
    Creation Magazine, volume 19, issue 1.
    www.answersingenesis.org/creation/v19/i1
    /lostworld.asp?vpriny=1.

Chapter 13

Allen, Thomas B. "The Silk Road's Lost World."
    National Geographic. March, 1996.
Barber, Elizabeth Wayland. *The Mummies of
    Urumchi.* New York, W.W. Norton and
    Company, 1999.
Ellis, Elisabeth Gaynor. *World History:
    Connections to Today.* Upper Saddle River,
    New Jersey, Prentice Hall, 2001.

Fletcher, Joann. "From Chile to China...Mummies Around the World." *http://www.bbc.co.uk/history/ancient/egyptian/mummies_06.shtml*. September 1, 2001.

Lynch, David J. "In Xinjiang Province, an Uneasy Coexistence." *USA Today*. September 23, 2004. p. 15A

Mair, Victor. *The Tarim Mummies: Ancient China and the Mystery of the Earliest Peoples From the West*. New York: Thames and Hudson, 2000.

Malkovich, John. "Riddle of the Desert Mummies." *Discovery Channel* documentary, 1998.

Marotta, Paul. "Mummy Dearest: 'Mysterious Mummies of Asia' on Nova." News Release issued by *Nova/WGBH*, 1998. http://sciencedaily.com/releases/1998/01/980107084900.htm.

O'Brien, Ellen. "Mystery of the Mummies." The *Philadelphia Inquirer*. 1996. http://sln.fi.edu/inquirer/mummy.html

Pringle, Heather. "Secrets of the Red-Headed Mummies." from the *Mummy Congress*. http://www.geocities.com/j_chandler21/mummies.htm. September 30, 2003.

Reid, Howard. "Mysterious Mummies of China." *PBS Nova* documentary, 1998.

Rosof, Libby. "Penn Researcher Finds Chinese Mummies' Surprising Roots." 9/9/07 – Alamanac, vol. 44, no.3, pg. 12-13. *http://www.upenn.edu/pennnews/current/features/1997/090997/mummies.html*.

Chapter 14

Cashill, Jack. "Clinton Blocked Truth About Murdered U.S. Troops." *www.worldnetdaily.com.* Oct. 5, 2004.

Cashill, Jack. "Clinton Covered up 1996 Atlanta Olympic Bombings." *www.worldnetdaily.com.* Oct. 19, 2004.

Cashill, Jack. "History Channel Blows Holes in Fed's TWA 800 Story." *www.worldnetdaily.com.* Oct. 11, 2004.

Cashill, Jack. "Mega Fix: The Dazzling Political Deceit That Led to 9/11." DVD Documentary, Outpost Pictures, 2004.

Cashill, Jack. "The Oklahoma City Aftermath." *www.worldnetdaily.com.* September 24, 2004.

Cashill, Jack. "The Oklahoma City Bombing." *www.wnd.com.* September 21, 2004.

Cashill, Jack. "TWA Flight 800: Attacked, Destroyed, Covered-Up." *www.worldnetdaily.com.* Oct. 7, 2004.

CNN.com. "Google Bows to Chinese Censorship." September 27, 2004.

Hutzler, Charles. "China Finds New Ways to Restrict Access to the Internet." *The Wall Street Journal.* 9-1-2004.

Liang and Xiangsui. *Unrestricted Warfare: China's Master Plan to Destroy America.* Panama City, Panama: Pan American Publishing Company, 2002. (originally published in 1999 by China's People's Liberation Army, Beijing).

Navrozov, Lev. "U.S. Losing Nanoweapons Race to China." *www.newsmax.com.* July 16, 2004.

Spencer, Robert. "Horowitz Exposes Leftist's Radical Islam Connection." *Human Events.* October 4, 2004. pg. 20

"My people are destroyed from lack of knowledge..."

Hosea 4:6

Book Order Form

- ❑ Please rush me _____ copy/copies of *Suppressed History II: Pulverizing Politically Correct Paradigms.*
- ❑ Please rush me _____ copy/copies of the original *Suppressed History: Obliterating Politically Correct Orthodoxies.*

Name: _____

Address: _____

City: _____ State:____

Zip code:_____

When ordering *Suppressed History*, send a check or money order for $14.95 plus $3.00 shipping to Armistead Publishing, P.O. Box 54516, Cincinnati, OH 45254, or pay by credit card.

Visa or MasterCard Number:

_____

Expiration Date:

_____

Quantity Discounts: Choose any combination of 5 books for $60.00, or 10 books for $99.99, plus $3.00 shipping.